First Steps in Secondary Teaching

From Survival to Confidence

Herbert K. Heger

University of Kentucky
and
Louisville Urban Education Center

Charles E. Merrill Publishing Company
A Bell & Howell Company
Columbus, Ohio

To Julie
Who, as loving wife and school teacher,
supported my perspective

Published by
Charles E. Merrill Publishing Company
A Bell & Howell Company
Columbus, Ohio 43216

International Standard Book Number: 0-675-08955-7

Library of Congress Catalog Card Number: 73-75052

Printed in the United States of America

Preface

This volume is designed to assist the pre-service teacher in understanding the problems he will face in adjusting to professional reality. Whether used in a methods class or in connection with direct experiences, this volume aims to lessen the shock of the first days of teaching. It will assist the pre-service teacher in identifying the unfinished tasks he faces. It will raise questions, issue challenges, and suggest directions the student may pursue and techniques he may use in becoming a mature professional. This text offers the professor a means of practicing what he preaches by involving his students more dynamically than is usually possible.

It will be helpful to note the unusual format of this volume. A mixture of readings, problems, problem response pages, and structured group activities, this volume is intended to provide a stimulus for active classroom interaction about a series of problems and issues which are arranged in a thematic order.

"Adjusting to Reality" is the first theme. Here the student is made aware of the nature and scope of the task facing the novice educator, and he is asked to ponder and respond to a series of problems illustrating the depth and severity of the challenge of reality.

"Achieving Success" is the theme in Chapters 3 and beyond. The student is presented with elements of teaching which will assist him in developing a personal strategy for coping with the problems presented earlier. He will be able to examine and test exemplars for successful teaching. Through active involvement, the student will begin to build confidence as well as competence in teaching.

Most of the principles and activities presented here have been developed by the author in his secondary methods classes with the active support of his students. Their suggestions and criticisms were vital to the development of this book. The authors whose articles are included here have assisted the author in creating a broader perspective than is usually possible Mrs. Connie West labored many hours typing the manuscript. This book would not have been feasible without assistance of all these people.

Herbert K. Heger

Contents

Introduction

Your Concerns as a Novice Teacher

From your very first day in the classroom, you will be expected to function as a professional. The eighth-grade girl who has just been roughed up by a ninth-grade boy will expect you to assist her. It does not matter how inexperienced you are; the need and challenge are exactly the same. If you have not had prior experience with problems of this sort, you may be ineffective due to the shock and uncertainty of the confrontation. Your charge in the next chapter, "Adjusting to Reality," is to ponder the real world of teaching and to develop some tentative hypotheses about appropriate personal teaching strategies. You will be able to test, extend, and refine these strategies in later chapters and in other portions of your pre-service education. By undertaking this challenge seriously, you will become more confident in your ability to cope with reality. The sooner you learn to survive in a classroom, the sooner you can get down to the business of teaching children.

In one school where the author taught, a certain biology teacher always introduced himself at the start of the school year by saying, "I am John Jones and I teach children." Every year the rest of the faculty would laugh at John, for they were teaching English, mathematics, or some other subject. Mr. Jones was deeply committed to the idea that he existed to serve his students while many of his colleagues thought he was odd. Too many of his fellow professionals existed to serve a discipline.

For decades educators have paid lip service to teaching the "whole child," but it was not until late in the sixties that the good intentions of teachers were put to the test. Parents as well as students are now *demanding* that educators get down to the business of dealing with individual students as people.

You probably agree with the new humanistic concern for students as people and fully intend to avoid the mistakes of your predecessors in education. This is easier said than done. Frances Fuller's study of teachers provides chilling evidence of the problems

1

facing pre-service teachers and their professors.[1] According to her study, teacher concerns fall into three broad categories, personal survival as a teacher, developing better content, and meeting the needs of students. During the pre-service period and the first year or so of professional involvement, the first priority of teachers is personal survival. Later the teachers' first concern seems to be with the content to be taught. Only after about the fifth year of teaching does the first concern of teachers focus on the needs of their students.

In this era it is very likely that a teacher cannot survive until he learns how to handle student concerns, yet the paradox is that he seems to be unable to worry about others until he first can survive. Arthur Jersild develops this same point in his book, "When Teachers Face Themselves."[2] In layman's terms, he says teachers need to be free of hangups about themselves before they can teach.

This text attempts to resolve this dilemma by compressing the time between survival and commitment to others. The approach is to bring you face to face with problems of the real world while you are still in the relatively secure atmosphere of college by providing you with certain techniques which are not usually available to beginning teachers. Hence, the theme of this book, "From Survival to Confidence."

One cannot give answers to people who have no questions. The first portion of this text aims to confront the student teacher with reality in order to provide a motivation for learning the methods to be developed later. The author hopes that the first part of the text will raise many questions in your mind.

Great reliance in the first part of this text is placed upon first person reports of the nature of contemporary reality and upon activities designed to involve you in active role play and discussion of the real-world demands you will face.

In the second part of this text the focus is on the kind of instructional techniques which can help you, as a new teacher, actively involve students. The assumption is made that the greatest need of beginning teachers is twofold: how to create instructional plans and materials that get high school students to participate, and how to make their activities fit into a traditional school structure. Simulation, gaming, and role play have been selected as the prime media in meeting the above criteria because these methods permit the young teacher not only to observe his students at work but to learn about them as people.

Teaching the Total Child: What's Involved?

In spite of the efforts of educators, four facts remain outstanding in the current American school.

1. The health of the home has a greater impact on the life and growth of a child than the school.

---

[1] Frances Fuller, "Concerns of Teachers: A Developmental Conceptualization," *American Education Research Journal* VI, no. 2, (March 1969), 207–26.

[2] Arthur Jersild, *When Teachers Face Themselves* (New York: Teachers College press, Columbia University, 1955).

2. Within the school the teacher's personality makes more difference than any other factor or group of factors.
3. Most graduates of American schools make their real impact on society in an area outside of the planned curriculum.
4. The school system itself is a battleground (rather than a place to learn) in an inexcusably large number of places.

It seems quite clear that there is a factor or set of factors beyond the planned curriculum which makes great difference to the child. There is something beyond the content of course work, beyond the conventional classroom processes, which make all the difference. The issues are "What can I as a teacher do about it?" and "How can I gain confidence and competence to do it?"

The Critical Omissions in Public School Curricula

Think for a moment about the famous and infamous people of the world. How did they make their impact on society? What skills did they use? Where did they learn these skills? Did the school have a role in shaping their abilities? Did the real influence of the school fall within the planned curricula or outside of the intended message of school?

An example, perhaps overly dramatic, may clarify the point. It has been widely reported that Presidents Truman and Kennedy were not outstanding students, yet both made powerful constructive contributions to society. In the case of President Truman, one notes how he possessed the ability to master any challenge and how he could grow while under fire. Nowhere in the planned curriculum can one find planned units relating to the development of such abilities.

President Kennedy was a masterful scholar, yet he did not produce a scholarly academic record at Harvard; he left his mark outside of the classroom. Fortunately, presidents are not chosen by college major and grade point average. There is no doubt but that the one important factor in John F. Kennedy's background was his unique family heritage. In retrospect, it is easy to observe that the skills he exercised in the Cuban missile crisis or on the campaign trail were not related to the official school curriculum.

Sirhan Sirhan, convicted of the assassination of the dynamic Senator Robert Kennedy, was also a graduate of American schools. Did American education fail to give Sirhan the skills necessary to become a positive rather than a negative force? One must conclude that the curriculum Sirhan experienced did not treat certain vital areas which were, in fact, a part of his total personality; school did not give him certain personal adjustment skills.

Schools have tended to deal in isolated facts instead of relationships, in memorization instead of application and reinforcement. Further, schools have tended to restrict their concern to the cognitive domain in spite of widespread recognition that there are equally important areas of concern outside of that realm.

There are few researched answers which tell educators how to handle these shadowy areas. Indeed, we are not even completely certain how to handle the cognitive domain.

Since we cannot stop teaching while such researched answers are being prepared, the trend has been to ignore that which we do not understand.

One would expect that with such a difficult challenge teachers would receive adequate professional support and assistance. Sadly, such support has seldom existed, and the teacher works alone nearly all the time. Is support likely to be available in the future? The future of education is uncertain, and its current problems are manifold:

1. Schools are expected to cope with most of the ills of society, from drug abuse to moral training.
2. The majority of teachers fail to remain in the profession. Many of the professional dropouts leave because they cannot cope with the challenge. While figures vary from university to university, it is often estimated that only one-third of teacher education graduates are teaching by the fourth year after graduation.
3. Teachers on the firing line no longer look to the administration for assistance and reward. Increasingly, the National Education Association and the American Federation of Teachers have become militant in their demands. Strikes are no longer unusual.
4. Students are becoming more rowdy and militant.
5. Defeats of financial proposals, from local bond issues to state and federal aid proposals, are common.

The trends are not clear, but the air of crisis within American schools is clear. The seriousness of the challenge of adjusting to reality cannot be underestimated.

The problem of the new teacher, then, amounts to this: *"In the face of inadequate knowledge and insufficient resources to assist me in moving forward in my professional skills, my very survival as a teacher demands that I gain competence and confidence in dealing with the total human condition. How do I cope with the challenge?"*

Adjusting to Reality

The View of a "New Teacher"

A recent graduate describes an experience he calls "the ongoing trauma of the brand new white teacher in an all-black junior high school in North Philadelphia." The scope of the challenge to the new teacher is defined in the following article, "New Teacher," by Reed Hundt.[1]

> Teaching in my school is like being in an obscure play which has been running for several years. There are thousands of actors who all look and act the same. There are several scenes and we repeat them over and over pointlessly. There is no audience and all the actors work very hard. It looks like a comedy but there is no laughter.
>
> Perhaps a scenario is more expressive: 35 kids run into the teacher's room. Some are depressed, some are manic. They fight, talk, yell, sharpen pencils, go to the nurse, yell, talk, fight. At a bell 43 minutes later, they run out. Repeat eight times a day for the kids, five times for teacher. By 3:30 closing time kids seem likely to die if they cannot escape; teachers desire either to destroy the entire public school system or to rearrange simply one face of one kid who said one unforgiveable word that day.
>
> Perhaps facts describe it better. There are 2,000 kids in grades 7–9 stacked five floors up on one city block. Of the approximately 750 seventh graders arranged in 22 different sections, about 75 could read on grade level at the beginning of the year. At most one-fourth of my school's children will graduate from high school, and at best one-tenth will go to college. A few will even be killed as they struggle through his progression of failure: a majority of the 42 gang killings in Philadelphia last year occurred within a few miles' radius of my school. There is an aura of timelessness about my school. I find it

---

[1]Reprinted with permission from the June 1970 issue of the *Yale Alumni Magazine;* copyright by Yale Alumni Publications, Inc.

5

especially hard to believe that just last year I was concluding my time at Yale
with a psycho-history paper; now I think I am living a psycho-history called
"The ongoing trauma of the brand-new white teacher in an all-black junior
high school in North Philadelphia."

I have 170 seventh graders for five social studies classes supposedly studying world geography. In reality, we undergo together a series of experiences
concerning the supposed authority of the teacher vs. the presumed rights of
the student, the necessity of achieving a sitting posture and a low noise level
to learn, the physio-psychological adjudication of internal class difficulties,
full volume speaking, and, on sporadic occasions, reading and map work.

More and more Yale students are going through this experience: the uni-
versally labeled "horrible first year of teaching" in an urban black school. In
the Class of 1960, 22 men out of 900 went immediately into teaching; in my
class 1969, this number more than tripled. And according to Assistant Yale
College Dean Donald H. Akenson, most of these draft deferment-seeking,
public service-minded students go to urban public schools. The experience
undoubtedly shakes them all.

The first shock for Yale graduates seeking public school jobs is that the
world does not want them as much as they might have guessed. Public schools
require education credits—some few farsighted students take such courses
before graduation, but most can only promise school boards that they will
attend night school after being hired.

I looked for jobs in Chicago, St. Louis, Boston, suburban Massachusetts,
New York City, Los Angeles, Philadelphia, New Orleans, and Washington,
D.C. Most school boards could not offer employment because of the education credits problem; others said I could earn the credits in summer school
or night school but they would not know about final job openings until Labor
Day, when they would discover how many teachers returned to the wars after
summer vacation. By then, of course, I would be drafted into a different war.

Fortunately, in August, soon after receiving my 1–A, I was given a post
in Philadelphia, which has few initial credit requirements. I joined at least
nine other members of my class going to teach in the Quaker City.

The typical Yale liberal arts graduate has a special problem in finding a
teaching job—his training does not suit schools' demands. Arnold Moss,
assistant director of personnel for the Philadelphia Board of Education, sum-
marizes the situation: "We have too many social studies and English appli-
cants for secondary positions. We are constantly in need of mathematics,
vocal music, women's physical education, and special education teachers.
And we always need elementary school teachers."

I was a social studies secondary school applicant because I thought the little
kids of elementary school would be unbearable. And I was sure that no matter
what they said about needs they would always want an Ivy League graduate.

But now I have changed my mind on many matters. Elementary school
might be much more satisfying than junior high school. Ivy League graduates

may not even be desirable in the teaching business. And no matter what you are or where you teach, the first year is going to be generally terrible.

Every new teacher—certainly every new white teacher—is mentally, emotionally, and physically blitzed by the experience of the black ghetto school. Arnold Moss says he tells liberal arts graduates they are "not prepared for teaching in an urban system." He tells them, "you can come in with all the enthusiasm in the world, but if you have no idea what to do, it's going to be hard." If his recruits are like me, they smile seriously and nod intently, meanwhile assuming their dedication, skills, and strength are greater than he conceives.

The first day is not so bad. Sitting behind the teacher's desk facing the orderly rows of empty seats, one imagines the pleasure of holding power over young minds. Writing the teacher's name on the board and finding it to be your own, one feels the thrill of holding a professional position in the world. And when the first kids enter—hushed, attentive, docile—one is happy to be able to seat them alphabetically in rows; it is as if order were being created out of chaos. It is downhill after that.

The first day I was told ways to maintain a "good learning situation" in my class. Put several vocabulary words or simple problems on the board to copy—this is called "pre-class work." It is designed to calm down the children and direct their thoughts toward learning. Seat everyone in order—boys on the wall side and girls on the window side. Last year, I was told, one teacher did not keep the boys on their side. Thus they threw a chair out of the window. The boy in it barely escaped a four-floor drop to the pavement. The teacher, I was told, did not believe in discipline, which was apparently a mistake.

But that first day my kids, all new to junior high school, passively and unexpectedly submitted to the traditional system: they took assigned seats and read the rules I had written on the board—do not chew gum, leave seat, touch windows or shades, or talk out in class. It would be a day or two before the system and I, its new lackey, were challenged.

I did not know how to teach or what to teach. The book was unreadable, so I mimeographed notes and tried to lecture on geographical terms and climate with my voice, hands, drawings, pictures, books, anything. My students absorbed little through the effort of lessons, and rudimentary discipline exhausted me. Gradually, difficulties in communication and control escalated. As soon as the kids realized their new school was like all schools, they were ready to educate me in the new realities of my "teaching-learning situation."

In a short time I realized everything I previously assumed about learning or schools was inaccurate in my new context. (See table.)

I realized things had changed when the Moratorium Committee announced the November march on Washington. Friday was to be a day of national holiday, a work stoppage to protest the war. At my school it was an occasion for the seventh graders to willfully misinterpret what news of the Moratorium

Shifting Perceptions of Mr. Hundt

Old Concepts	New Realizations
1. Books, even school books, are to be read.	1. Books are too hard to read, easier to throw, rip, stomp, ignore.
2. Pencils are to write with.	2. Pencils are to take and have taken. Pencils are to sharpen. Pencils are to throw. Pencils are in any of the above functions also to serve as instigators of mini-riots between two or more "students" at any time.
3. Mouths are to speak and discuss.	3. Mouths are to chew and smack gum with, to yell with.
4. Hands are to hold things and raise in class.	4. Hands are to slap or hit with, in hope of creating transitory but hilarious and ubiquitous disturbance.
5. Honkie is just a fun word au courant in liberal/radical sets.	5. Honkie is like Nigger, only it refers to white-skinned minorities. It usually is not meant humorously.
6. Teachers are to be treated with some respect.	6. Teachers are to taunt, abuse, and disregard.
7. A teacher is supposed to teach.	7. A teacher is psychophysical therapist handling a large number of cases who possess widely fluctuating abilities and dispositions, individually and as a group varying manically from day to day and moment to moment as mood strikes.
8. Disruptive students are to be treated quickly and professionally, with the aid of counselors and special education.	8. Disruptive students are to be: a. Recognized as often in the majority b. Yelled at, pushed, shoved or hit c. Sent to the isolation room, counselor, or vice-principal in hopes of finding a good disciplinarian in one of these offices. d. Ignored.
9. Teaching can be rewarding.	9. Teaching in the first year is physically, mentally, and emotionally a miserably exhausting job.

managed to seep through the Philly barrage of radio and TV reports of gang killings and traffic accidents. Somehow the 23 sections of seventh graders allowed themselves to hear the school was cancelled.

Meanwhile several war protesting teachers did not go to work that day. This action, so laudable among college faculty, amounted to desertion of duty according to the principal. (Remember: "A principal is your pal, a principle is what he yells about.") The administration played warden and the teachers police guards, but restlessness and rebellion mounted all day until during one class change several hundred seventh graders bolted for the doors. They were stopped, dispersed, and sent to their rooms/cells. We "professionals" (teachers) survived, but barely, and no thanks to the protesting teachers who did not show up.

By November I was into the routine of my school. The class—34 on rolls, 30 in school, 26 attending—enters as a thin, tardy screaming line of kids spread over the first 20 minutes of the 43-minute period. Once all are settled, several decide to begin disruptions. Causes: pencil stealing, slaps in the face, saying something about somebody's mother, random wandering about the room. Result: All watch disrupter, learning stops.

On days when I feel strong, my response is to smile, cheerfully breaking up continually recurring fights, and confidently await disturbances—perhaps a false alarm fire drill or a visitation from a group of marauding ninth graders or any of a million other possible incidents. On days I feel irritable or tired, I snap out, yell, push, hit. Then everyone is left turned-off and unimpressed. I resolved not to fail. In the early days one of the old "strong" teachers gave me some advice, "I just want to tell you what an old teacher told me when I started in this profession. They are just kids and you're a man." But everyone else kept telling me that the first year was hell for all teachers. I reminded myself I was a man, but that did not convince me that hell was an ideal place to prove the point.

Everything would have been easier if I had been born a perfect authoritarian/disciplinarian and if every kid in the school knew I was "hard." But I was not even convinced of the merit of the rules I wrote on the board the first day. Once the kids discovered this—it took about a week—they knew I was someone they could run over.

Of course, it really did not matter that I wavered on the rules because I could not enforce them in any case. Every day more and more infractions went ignored, and worse and worse grew the chaos. The number of individual teacher-student confrontations was high all fall. I had set myself up as an authoritarian (albeit a poor one), and therefore I was bound to be brought down.

Through the fall every kid who wanted to challenge me had his chance. In October I decided that it was right to hit kids on selected occasions. My homeroom vice president had stayed after school to convince me to employ corporal punishment. He wanted the kids to "act right" so he could learn something. That night I practiced slapping on a broom in my kitchen.

The next day I purposely and accurately hit one kid in each of my five sections and one extra in one section. Later, I applied the same technique to other students. It served me well very briefly. But then the tough kids arose and challenged me, wanting to be attacked in order to show how hard they were. Sometimes I obliged with a slap or push; they responded by "swaggering" about the room, yelling, cursing, putting up their hands for a fight. The end result was entertainment for the class, anger and frustration for me, internal turmoil for my antagonist. No one gained a thing.

One kid eventually reported me to the principal, and I received a note ordering the cessation of my corporal punishment program. I got angry and hit out again later—I even slapped a girl in one fit of fury—but the planned physical discipline ended. It was illegal, ineffective, and it left me unhappy. So now when I'm called "stupid" or "honkie" or whatever, I yell or look hurt; I know most of the kids too well to usually do more than shove them now.

Other teachers did not stop hitting. The principal is now being threatened with a law suit because one of his employees knocked a child cold. This teacher may be fired but corporal punishment will continue. The kids fight too much to expect the teachers to remain calm. The point, however, is that the teachers who have respect and status can get away with it; the new young teachers will fail at corporal punishment just as they fail at teaching.

Of course, the strongest and best of the teachers in my school—mostly adult blacks and a handful of young experienced whites—rarely hit kids and are effective teachers. But most teachers never attain effectiveness; my junior high school replaces half of its 95-man faculty every year.

Most new teachers fail partly because they cannot maintain the authoritarian/disciplinarian image that the experienced teachers project. Yet the system demands that this be the standard image of the teacher. It is everywhere assumed that the teacher is the final authority in the classroom. I heard one disciplinarian tell one of my kids who was in trouble, "you have got to understand that you are always wrong and the teacher is always right." Even teachers who listen to kids and respond to their desires still presume that in the end the teacher's word ought to be regarded as law. When new teachers make this assumption, the children refuse to accept it. The new teacher fails to be what he has defined himself to be, so he fails in his job.

A few times each week I wonder if the system has to be this way. Once I heard intelligent, experienced black teachers defend this authoritarian system: "You have to have a very structured, rigid system in which a kid can find his place easily. I do not approve of this. It perpetrates exactly the kind of enslavement of blacks which I am totally opposed to. But it is necessary. If you give him too much freedom, the kid is lost."

Perhaps this teacher is right, if you accept the system's definition of being lost. The system is designed to perpetuate certain standards of so-called education and so-called good behavior.

If the system was designed for individual teachers and individual students to determine their ways of operating and learning, it would have a chance of overall success. The way it is now, only a few can succeed; and in the process the sacrifices of individual integrity to both teachers and students are enormous.

This failure of teachers perpetuates itself because there are not enough experienced teachers to keep the system working in an orderly fashion. There are 12,800 teachers in Philadelphia public schools; more than 5,000 have been hired in the past three months. One-third of the faculty leaves each year. Draft dodgers reach 26; young women marry and become pregnant; and others just cannot stand the strain and frustration.

In 1967 the school board, led by former Philadelphia Mayor Richardson Dilworth, decided to make the best of the situation by recruiting the best possible young teachers, no matter how long they were expected to stay. If the turnover was going to be high, they reasoned at least a high-quality stream of recruits would be passing through Philadelphia schools.

There has been some criticism of their results. "Philadelphia Magazine," a local liberal monthly, ran an article in October entitled "The Artful Dodgers," condemning the influence of teachers who joined the profession temporarily, half out of interest and half out of draft necessity:

"In front of a class . . . removed from the occupations they were trained for, [the draft-dodging teachers] remain alienated and disenchanted. Unfortunately, their disenchantment often results in poor teaching, and the recipients of this below par teaching are Philadelphia's school children. Members of the Draft Dodger Corps don't seem to care. To say they could use a little more dedication would be an understatement.

"Even the darling of Ivy School liberals, John Gardner, has made related comments concerning the efficacy of the well educated in urban situations: The tasks of social change are tasks for the tough-minded and competent. Those who come to the task with the currently fashionable mixture of passion and incompetence only add to the confusion."

If there is anything I am sure I have accomplished, it is to add to the confusion. And maybe Philadelphia feels this is true of many Ivy League teachers; for because of budgetary reasons and probably wariness of my type of recruit, the personnel office has not yet found time to schedule visits to Yale or Princeton. Arnold Moss, assistant director, says he is recruiting "at schools where we feel prospects are high for getting good, qualified individuals." Translated, that means that the 20 who came from Harvard, Yale, and Princeton this fall do not, in number or in quality, justify special recruiting efforts at those schools. It is far more worthwhile to look for blacks from Morgan State or Virginia State or Norfolk State; a system that has 60 percent Negro pupils and only 25 percent Negro teachers needs black faculty more than Ivy B.A.'s. And Moss and the others in his office can recruit more blacks for inner city teaching at Temple than at an Ivy school. Anyone who thinks 10 recruits from Yale is a large figure should remember that 300 to 350 teachers come out of Temple every year.

Of course, no matter where new teachers come from they will have a bad time for the first year. But at least by the end of the fall the fighting will generally stop. After a few months nothing will surprise the teacher, and nothing the teacher does will seem quite so foreign and threatening to the students. With many students, real rapport and friendships will develop. I enjoy most of my kids; many have already undergone so many hard and harrowing experiences at home and in the street that you could respect no one more. From the kids—the students, basketball players, fighters, and diplomats—the teacher can enjoy learning.

Appreciating the qualities of the kids leads, of course, to greater frustration. The fact is that no more than a handful of my 170 students will ever escape their depressing environment. There is no room to grow in the poverty-stricken ghettos of North Philadelphia. Blocks and blocks of row houses pour legions of children into the streets and schools to ply together in packs so tight that every person has to develop amazing personality defenses just to give himself breathing space. Thus even conversation is often hostile, boasting, and aggressive. And energy can never be harmlessly exerted in open space; rather it is always directed toward other people so that during the day a class will make itself more and more volatile until explosions of fights and yelling ease the pressure. It hurts to fail to teach these children. School should be one way to escape the ghetto; instead it is one of the conditions of the trap. And although few ever achieve the good life that school is constantly promising, most are deceived into believing that school work will get them somewhere. "Do the work"—this is an acknowledged virtue at my school and the special accomplishment of the "good" kids who have blindly or intelligently followed teacher's orders. The work may consist of copying from the board or from a book, reading a mimeographed paper, or doing a test—it matters little if it involves learning. It is only necessary that it be done. Of course in my class this hoax is less successful: the noise and disruption is so constant that even "The Work" usually goes undone.

Non-teaching is the new teacher's lot the first year and is concomitant with the noise that indicates what the system calls "failure to maintain discipline." And some discipline failure is almost unavoidable the first year. It is impossible to become an authoritarian overnight. But this simply should not be a requirement of becoming a teacher.

A book by Herbert Kohl called *The Open Classroom* expresses another way of teaching. In the traditional authoritarian classroom, Kohl argues, the teacher is one army and the students another—they wage physical and spiritual warfare over the battlefield of subject matter. Usually all are wounded and neither makes any real advances. This system is implicit or overly present in most classrooms in this country. In contraposition, Kohl offers the idea of the open classroom. The class learns as a group of individuals, not as a subjected colony. The teacher avoids seating charts, grading systems, and all the traditional demands of control over children's individual rights. Everyone is a free individual—and respect for this fact is the greatest lesson of the open classroom.

This room is almost impossible to achieve. It requires the teacher to make all experiences contribute to the desired atmosphere of group learning. In elementary school one might almost have the time to accomplish this utopian goal. But the junior high school's insanely rigorous schedule; its corridors; fights and fleecings; its artificial separation of three mismatched grades; in short, its systematic development of insensitivity, all seem to preclude development of open classrooms.

The junior high school is so absurd that authoritarianism seems the only way to force at least some logic into the situation. It may be the logic of a mad bureaucrat, but at least it is not anarchy. The problem, however, is that the school system has great difficulty in maintaining the regulations of authoritarianism. And when that breaks down, as it has in many of my classes, there is no trust or friendship to rely on. It makes you long for the docile passivity of affluent and dead suburbs.

At least my kids are aggressive and experienced and alive. In fact, their aggressive vitality is approximately that of an earthquake. But whether you sit on an earthquake or let it explode around you, it is difficult to teach in. The struggle every day leaves me tired, my kids tired, my school tired, the whole system tired. Someday everyone and everything might collapse from exhaustion. But more likely all will continue to plod along, crippling and conforming, condemning and commending children, instead of educating them.

Maybe the system can be changed. And perhaps trying to change it would only destroy it. In any case all console me by promising that teaching improves a great deal the second year, but I cannot figure out whether that is a recommendation to stay or not.

To anybody who is planning on going through the same experience, I wish good luck. You better believe everything the recruiting pamphlets say about the occupation being a challenge.

Problem 1

1–1. (Individual)

Some would say that the difficulties encountered by Mr. Hundt are related to his discipline problems. It should be easy to recognize that discipline is only symptomatic of deeper problems in his school.

List five kinds of basic problems which went untreated in Mr. Hundt's school:

1–2. (Individual)

What can a teacher do about these problems?

1–3. *(Discussion Groups of Four)*

Discuss what teachers can do about these problems.

1–4. *(Discussion Groups of Four)*

How can a teacher teach while these problems exist?

1–5. *(Individual)*

How do the problems in suburban schools differ from the ones described by Mr. Hundt?

1–6.   (Individual)

What suburban problems are similar to Mr. Hundt's problems?

1–7.   (Discussion Groups of Four)

Try to identify suburban problems similar to Mr. Hundt's.

From the Principal's Office

Mr. Hundt was not presenting an unusual case. Here is the view from the principal's office in another city. This is a difficult school in the city involved, but not unusual or unique on the national scene. One May principals from a Midwest city system exchanged positions briefly with a number of professors and administrators from the College of Education at the Ohio State University. The idea grew out of long-time collaboration between the city system and Ohio State in the preparation of teachers.

Luvern Cunningham, Dean of the College of Education, had volunteered for the exchange and was assigned to what is generally regarded as the most difficult school in the cooperating system. He frankly confesses that the experience was a revelation —a useful one, however—and in this report[2] he tells about it as he saw it. (At the request of administrators in the cooperating system, its identity is withheld.)

This is a report. It is as objective as I can make it. The remarks that follow are based on a few days' experience as principal of an inner-city junior high school—a problem-saturated place.

I want it known that although what I say here is critical, it is not intended to be critical of any person or group of persons. But it is an indictment of us all—educators and laymen, critics and the criticized.

The notion of an exchange cropped up out of the woodwork. Someone had an idea that this would be a good thing to do. The big-city people agreed and we agreed and so we were off and running. We didn't have the luxury of much advanced planning time. Had we had a chance to contemplate the event in Columbus (in the peace and quiet and solitude of the ivory tower) we could have lost our courage and copped out on the whole deal. We didn't have that time, so we did appear at our respective schools at the appointed hour, Monday, May 5. On that fateful morning (like little kids going to kindergarten) we picked up our pencil boxes and marched off to the school house.

I arrived at about 7:45 A.M. I had read about the city's riots in 1966 and I knew it was near here that they had started. I was aware too that this was a junior high that had been having its share of trouble. I knew that the faculty stayed away for two days, saying that this school was an unfit place in which to carry on professional activity.

My first several minutes as the new helmsman were exciting, to say the least. I walked in through the front door and introduced myself to the regular principal's secretary. She was most cordial and smiled knowingly. I think she chuckled to herself, thinking that this guy is really in for an education. If those were her feelings she was quite right.

I walked into the office and was about to set my briefcase down. I looked up and there must have been 20 faces, most of them black, all around. And others were coming through the office door. Some were students, some were

[2]Luvern L. Cunningham, "Hey Man, You Our Principal? *Phi Delta Kappan* 51, no. 3 (November 1969). Reprinted by permission.

faculty members with students in tow, others were clerks who wanted me to make some monumental decisions about events of the day.

They weren't even in line. They were all just kind of standing around there competing for attention. And to make life more exciting a little black fellow with a flat hat and cane about two feet long came up to me. He whipped that cane around on his arm and stuck it in my stomach and said, "Hey, man, you our principal?" I began thinking longingly of Columbus and said, "Well, no, I'm not. But I'm here for a week and I am going to be taking his place." I was backpeddling and trying to think of some answer that would make sense to this eighth-grade student.

A number of youngsters who were crowding around were just curious; others had problems. One was a girl who had recently been released from a correctional institution and was under court order to come back to school. She was there for an appointment, but she didn't want to come back to this or any other school. She was openly hostile, asking harshly that she not be made to come back. I had no file. I didn't have any background on this young lady. I was unprepared to make a decision. So instead of displaying administrative genius, I said, "Would you sit down over there and I'll talk to you later." She sat—head down, sullen, oblivious to the confusion surrounding us. It was an hour before I got back to her problem.

There was tragedy and comedy. A teacher who was obviously disturbed about something had a very attractive 16-year-old girl by the hand. She came in and said, "I understand you're the new principal, Mr. Cunningham. Look at that skirt. Look at that mini-skirt. It's entirely too short. Just look at that thing. I think we ought to send her home. Aren't you going to send her home?"

She turned to the girl and said, "Is your mother home?" The girl said "No." "When will she be home?" "Well, she'll be home about 6:15 tonight."

The teacher turned to me and said, "We can't send her home." Then she marched the girl over in front of me, rolled that brief skirt up several inches and said, "Look at that, it's got a hem in it that long. We ought to be able to take that hem out. Let's go back to the classroom." I didn't have a chance to say a word.

In the meantime other kids were still clustered around. They had their own brand of problems so I said, "Would you go and wait outside the office please and come in one at a time?" They kept coming in with their questions, some that I could answer, most that I could not.

When the first bell rang and the students had to go to their homerooms, faces disappeared, the corridors cleared a bit, and there was an atmosphere of temporary calm. I was able to sit down and try to get my bearings. It was an inauspicious beginning, to say the least.

Let me comment a bit about Lester Butler. Lester was assigned to the principal's office. His responsibility was to be available during free periods for phone calls, delivery of messages, and any other tasks that might appropriately be handled by an eager, intelligent seventh-grader. After quiet had been established in the office on that first day he gave me a quick tour of the building. He took me to obvious places like the library, the auditorium, the gymnasium, and special classrooms, but he also pointed out the nooks and crannies, the special recesses, the hideaways of the old structure. With his special brand of radar he was able to track me down and bring messages to me during the week when I was about the building. We became unusually fine friends.

This junior high school building is old. The oldest part was built 65 years ago. It has had two additions. Despite its age the building has been refurbished from time to time; it was painted and the windows were in. It's not particularly unattractive from the inside, but as a structure to house education it's a nightmare of inefficiency. Traffic patterns are unbelievable. You have to go upstairs to get downstairs. You go upstairs across a kind of plateau and down the other side to reach another part of the building. The arrangements for science and home economics facilities, as well as classrooms housing other particular specialized aspects of the curriculum, do not accommodate decent traffic patterns. When the bell sounds and classes pass it is a wild place. It's wild in between times, too, for that matter.

The absentee rate is very high. Of the nearly 1,800 enrolled, between 350 and 400 were absent every day. Where they were no one really knows. There was no apparent relationship between my presence and the absentee rate; that's the way it is every day. During my first day a counselor took me in his car and just crisscrossed the neighborhood. He wanted to point out the housing, the neighborhood, the fact that the streets were crowded with humanity just milling around. It was a warm week, the first week in May. People were outside. Kids of all ages were all over. There appeared to be as many youngsters on the street as there were in the elementary school and junior and senior highs.

Ironically, everybody shows up during the lunch period. The lunches are partly financed with federal funds and the youngsters are admitted to the lunchroom by ticket. Kids who are truant get into the building (despite door guards) and into the cafeteria. They have something to eat and then melt into the community.

The building is a sea of motion—people are moving about all the time. Adults (teachers, teaching assistants, observers, student teachers, door guards, other people who get in through the doors despite the guards) and students are in the halls all the time. Some of the students have passes to go somewhere given by somebody, but most students are just there. Those who don't have passes have excuses. As a newcomer seeing all of this motion, what should I have done? Should I have gotten tough? Should I have tried to shout them back to class? Should I have threatened such and such? Or should I have turned my head and let them go on about their own purposes? I turned my head.

When I was in my office students would come in with all sorts of questions, grievances, or requests for excuses. Apparently the pattern in the building is that if you can't get a hearing for your complaint anywhere else you end up in the principal's office. I had a steady flow of customers.

The school has 85 teachers. There is a high absence rate each day among teachers too. They fail to show up for many reasons. The teacher absentee numbers (while I was there) would range from 11 to 14 per day. If you have a faculty of 85 and 14 teachers fail to show (and you don't get substitutes), you have to make some kind of ad hoc arrangements quickly to handle the crises. Each day three to five substitutes would appear and they would be assigned to cover classes. But they were not enough. Furthermore, there was little relation between the substitutes' teaching fields and their assignments. The first priority is to put live people in classes to maintain some semblance of order.

The youngsters, as I said, were in motion. I had the feeling that I was walking on a live volcano. Classes were often noisy and rowdy. Fights and squabbles broke out frequently. Fights between girls occurred about five to one more often than fights among boys. But the fights among the girls were often over boys. The adult population was on pins and needles from the time the building opened in the morning until school was out at 3:30 in the afternoon. Everyone hoped to make it through the day without large-scale violence.

The day is organized around eight periods. Students have a number of free periods, during which time they are assigned to study halls. Some go to a large auditorium; others go to classrooms with teachers assigned to study hall duty there. Large numbers congregate in the cafeteria on the ground floor for "study." The cafeteria accommodates around 300 youngsters. Teachers are reluctant to supervise the cafeteria study halls. When they do it is with fear and trembling. The place is noisy. Kids move around despite the efforts of several teachers to keep them seated. They shoot craps. Some play other games. There is bickering and fighting. Kids pick up chairs and fling them across the room at one another. It's dirty and hot.

The whole building is hot, because the custodians cannot shut off the heat. It is the only way to provide hot water for the lunch program. So they keep the stokers going to have hot water for the federally subsidized lunches. Everybody complains about it: the principal, the assistant principal, the teachers, the students, and the PTA.

The lunchroom study halls are unbearable. The undermanned custodial staff is unable to keep the table tops clean; a slimy film covers them. They are neither attractive for eating nor for study purposes. Because of the danger of intruders coming in off the streets, the major cafeteria emergency exit has been nailed shut. Teachers asked the principal to have the custodians do this. The custodians refused because of fire regulations. In desperation the principal himself nailed it shut. Every day he lives in fear that a fire will break out and students will be trapped. Large numbers might not get out through the narrow passageways that serve as entrances and exits. Thus a measure taken to protect the teachers could lead to another type of disaster.

We called the police only once during my stay. It was different at another junior high school where my colleague Lew Hess served as principal. At night following his first day a fire bomb was thrown through his office window. It was a dud and didn't go off. On his last day three fire bombs were thrown inside the building and they did go off. The police and fire department had to be summoned each time.

On the second day, in a classroom study hall right across from my office, a young boy was late. His name was Willy Denton. He was about a minute and a half tardy and his excuse was that he had been next door signing up for a special program of summer employment. The study hall supervisor had obviously had a hectic morning. As Willy entered the room a few words were exchanged. The supervisor grabbed Willy, put a hammerlock around his neck, kind of chocked him, and wrestled him out into the corridor. The noise attracted other kids. Immediately there were about 40 students as well as door guards right around the teacher and Willy. Willy got free for a moment but the supervisor caught him again, this time grabbing him by the shoulders. He shook him against the lockers and that was like whomping a big bass drum. The sound reverberated around that part of the building and more people came. The supervisor got a fresh hammerlock on Willy, dragged him over to my office, threw him in and across to the other side, and said, "Take charge."

I suppose that I turned whiter in that sea of black, but I took charge. I closed the door and asked Willy to sit down. All of a sudden another teacher opened the door about six inches and shouted, "Willy's got a good head on his shoulders," slammed the door, and left.

It was about 12 noon. The period had just started. There were nearly 35 minutes until Willy was to go to another class. So Willy and I just talked. I didn't think that lining him up for swats would make much difference. He was livid. If he had been white he would have been purple. He was furious, and so we just sat and talked.

We talked about what he liked and what he disliked. I asked him if he had worked last summer, since he was going to be employed this coming summer. He said that he had. I asked where and he said, "I worked in a church." And he added, "You know I teach Sunday School." I asked how old his class members were and he said, "Well they're about the same age as I am." "How many do you have?" "About 15, and sometimes I teach on Saturdays too." "Do you like to teach?" He said, "Well, it's okay. But boy those first Sundays my stomach just kind of turned around and I didn't know what I was doing. But it's better now. Like last Sunday, did you hear about that plane that was shot down in Korea? You know, we just talked about that. I sat down and we talked about that."

It was clear that Willy loved what he was doing in Sunday school. He liked math too and he planned to go to high school. But he was so angry at that study hall supervisor. He trembled for several minutes; he just couldn't get control. We talked through the balance of the hour till the bell rang. I sent him on to his next class sans swats.

The PTA leaders came in to meet with me on Wednesday. They shared their definitions of the school's problems. I held a faculty meeting on Thursday. And I was amazed at the similarity between faculty and parent sentiments on the issues facing the school.

The teachers, by and large, are a very dedicated lot. Many of them are young; some of them are coming out of MAT programs. Despite their youth they, like the rest of the faculty, are tired, disheartened, even despondent. But they don't want to fail.

One of the teachers was shot 10 days before I arrived on the scene. He missed his lunch break and went across the street to get a coke and a bag of potato chips. Coming back he was held up on the street and shot with a pellet gun. He came back into the building, walked into the principal's office, with his hand pressed against his side. Blood was spewing between his fingers and he said, "I'm shot, I'm shot, I'm shot." The principal called an ambulance and got him to the hospital. But he was back teaching while I was there, with the pellet still in him. He hadn't had time to have it taken out. He was going to the hospital that weekend to have the bullet removed.

I tried to visit classes and meet teachers. As I became known around the building, it was rather like walking down the hall and being attacked by aardvarks. Teachers would come out, grab me by the arm, pull me back into the teacher's lounge or their classrooms, and say, "Let me tell it like it is here." Every one of them had deep feelings for the school and for the kids, but an inability to define the specific changes that would make a difference. Their intense desire to solve the school's problems mixed with overwhelming despair is one of the powerful impressions that remains with me as a consequence of those days.

In many ways it is an overmotivated but underprepared staff. As one young fellow who came in March said, "This is an overpeopled and understaffed school. We've got lots of special people running around under federal grants doing their particular thing. But they don't fit into any kind of mosaic that has meaning for solving the problems of the school."

Many teachers have the too-little-and-too-late kind of feeling. No one is apologetic about it. There is no sense of humiliation about being assigned to the school. But most of them want to get out because they feel that it is an absolutely hopeless situation, that they can't afford to spend whatever psychic energy they have in fighting a losing battle. Even though they are emotionally committed to the place they still want to leave. So the turnover rate is high. Some youngsters had had several different teachers in some of their classes since the beginning of the year.

After the early chaos of my first morning I was able to visit a class being taught by a Peace Corps returnee. She was a young woman with an MAT degree. She had two adults with her in the room assisting with the youngsters. And it was pandemonium. She was trying to teach social studies. She was obviously searching desperately to locate something that might motivate or have some interest for 15 seventh-graders. Her Peace Corps assignment had been in Africa, so she was showing slides of how people construct thatched cottages there. It was something she knew about first-hand—she had been on the scene. But the kids tuned her out. They were making funny remarks and fighting.

One of the other adults in that room was a young man, a practice teacher who had arrived that morning. He had already been slugged twice by students before my 11 A.M. visit. I talked with him later in the week trying to find out whether he was going to give up or stick around. I had to admire his tenacity. He was going to stay; he wasn't going to be licked by that set of events.

During the lunch hour a group of seventh-grade teachers who were cooperating in a transitional program (transitional from the sixth grade into junior high) were meeting for a planning session. I was invited to sit in. The young Peace Corps returnee came in with a tear-stained face. She just couldn't manage her situation. She didn't know what to do. She had to go back and face those classes that afternoon and the next day and the next. She had been advised by the principal and by others to turn in her chips and move to another school. But she just wouldn't do it. She had been fighting it since September, facing failure all year long, but she just would not give up. Others like her were having similar experiences.

The curriculum at this junior high is archaic, outmoded, irrelevant, and unimportant in the minds of the kids who are there. The faculty has agreed for the most part that this is true. But no one is able to design a pattern of change which will remedy or act upon all of the deficiencies that are so prominent in the program of studies. Because of the way the building is constructed (room sizes, locations, and the like) they are locked into an eight-period day. There just are not enough classrooms to handle a six-period organization. Furthermore, there is ambiguity about who is responsible for curriculum reform. Everyone wants change but no one knows how to achieve it.

They were administering the Stanford Achievement Test the week I was there. Large numbers of kids couldn't read it. Many couldn't even read the name of the test. Some of them would mark all of the alternative responses; some wouldn't mark any; some would just casually draw pictures on the test; some would stare; others would raise their hands and ask for help from those who were monitoring the testing.

A few teachers raised the question with me, "Why test?" It is a good question. Or why use that kind of testing for youngsters in a junior high school like this one? Apparently standardized testing is a system-wide requirement which may have had historical significance and is continued merely because no one has considered not doing it.

As I have said, most of the teachers' energy goes into control. I found few classrooms where I could say with some confidence that there was excitement relative to learning. The only place where I saw interest and motivation and product was in home economics, which enrolls both boys and girls. In other areas interest and motivation appeared to be near zero. It seems to me that the traditional school "subjects" have to be very carefully analyzed in terms of some relevance criterion.

We toss that word around a great deal—relevance. It's in everybody's language. It has reached cliché status more rapidly than most similar words in our professional jargon. Nevertheless, there is some meaning there.

When I ask myself what would be relevant to the young people at this school I reach an impasse very quickly. It is hard to know what is relevant. Certainly it ties to motivation. If we were insightful enough to know what the prominent motivations are among such young people, then maybe we could organize a program of studies in keeping with interest areas. The program might look quite unlike the traditional subject-centered arrangement in these schools.

I mentioned earlier the "leakage" of the building, both inside out and outside in. The staff walkout in January, 1969, took place because the school was an unsafe place in which to teach. The Board of Education responded by putting door guards on the doors. The measure was to protect teachers and students from a range of intruder types. It was also to control students coming in and going out during the day. The guards have helped a bit in keeping invaders out of the building, but this move hasn't solved the pupil "leakage" of the building. An outsider (or an insider for that matter) will cause a disturbance at one of the doors. Door guards come quickly from their posts to help out, leaving their own stations unattended. Other kids will then open the unprotected doors and run out or run in, whichever suits their fancy.

Administrators and teachers resort to corporal punishment. The chief vehicle for control is the swat system. The teachers worked out a scheme to improve control following the January walkout. Teachers volunteer to help with discipline in the "gym balcony," a little area overlooking the gymnasium. During free periods kids who misbehaved, for whatever reason, are brought there. They queue up, outside, both boys and girls, waiting to be swatted. Teachers take their turns up there in the gym balcony. Similar disciplinary lineups occur outside of the office doors of the three assistant principals, who have paddles of razor straps hanging from their belts. If they need to use them in the corridors they do.

Disciplinary cases are brought first to their door. If they or the principal are too busy, in juvenile court or at home with a case of nerves or whatever it might be, then the students go to the gym balcony to get their swats. Afterward they go back to class or study hall or library to get out of the building.

I didn't administer corporal punishment. I don't know whether I was psychologically capable of it. I don't think I could have forced myself. Teachers on a few occasions brought students to my office. One teacher just threw them in, saying "Take charge" and leaving.

There doesn't seem to be any intrinsic motivation, any way of appealing to the interests of pupils to stay and learn. So everyone (adults and students) adjusts to the corporal punishment routine. No one likes it; no one wants it.

Teachers hate it; the principals hate it. But they have no other alternative. They have not been able to discover any better control measure.

And now about death. There is an astonishing callousness about death among the students here. One of them had been killed a few days earlier. He was shot in a car wash down the street. I have mentioned the shooting of the teacher; fortunately that did not end in death. There were other shoot-outs in the neighborhood ending in fatalities. Lester Butler, on my last day, sought an excuse to attend a funeral. I asked for particulars. He said, "It's for my friend's father. He was killed a week ago. He was shot right outside the school. I want to attend a funeral. I'll come right back after it's over." I wrote the excuse.

Lester described the event without emotion, with placidness, with matter-of-factness. Death is a part of life here. Life is filled with its own brand of violence. Its violence is routine. It is not necessarily racial. It is grounded in hate which feeds upon itself. It is cancerous and spreads and spreads and spreads.

The cancer of hate is latent within the student body. You sense its power. You sense its presence and the prospect for its release at any moment. You do not know when it will burst forth and cascade around you. It is every-where; it is nowhere. Lester sensed that the school was a powder keg. He would even try to describe it to me in his own way.

In many ways life at this junior high is a charade. People go about the business of routine schooling. Teachers laugh and smile. They walk through the corridors ignoring the rowdiness. They try at times, half-heartedly, to establish a bit of order. The administrative staff takes the problem more seriously; they shout and cajole and urge and plead. The counselors do their thing. They talk with students. They describe worlds of glitter and gold. The students squirm and stare and ignore. The counselors' cubicles, tucked away here and there, are temporary refuges from the storm.

I was impressed with the door guards. They try. They understand the charade. Many of them have played the game for a lifetime. They represent well the male image. They are for the most part young, strong, handsome. They are on the side of the angels. That is, they try to support the purposes of the school. They work closely with teachers and administrative officials. They do their job. It involves keeping hoodlums off the street out of the building, avoiding physical encounters but not turning away from them. There is no training for their positions. They must exercise amazing discretion every minute of the day. Most of them have little formal education. But they have established a bond with the professional staff that is harmonious and marked by mutual respect. Each day I issued up a silent prayer of thanks that they were there.

What to do about this school? And other similar junior highs in other places? An archaic building, a largely uncaring community, an irrelevant program of studies, a student population that is out of hand, an underpre-pared, overpressured staff, a sympathetic but essentially frustrated central administration, a city that wishes such schools would go away. A proposal from the staff and administrators was to burn the school down. Destroy it. Get the symbol out of the neighborhood. This was more than a half-serious proposal.

Short of that, what can be done? This question haunted me during my stay. What could be done? Only a few feeble proposals occurred to me.

I would argue for complete building-level autonomy. The principal and faculty should run the show without concern for other places. They should be allowed to organize the program of studies without adherence to district-wide curriculum guides and the like. The principal should be free to select his own faculty without reference to certification. He should look for talented people anywhere and everywhere. They could be found across the street or across the nation. The principal should build his own budget and make internal allocations in terms of the faculty and staff's definition of need.

More radically, I would ask that the principal be given complete control over time. That is, he should be able to open and close the school at will. If in his judgement events are getting out of hand, he should have the power —indeed be expected—to close the school down for a day, a week, or a month. During the time the building is closed, all of the adults in the school, in cooperation with students and community leaders, should focus on the problems that are overwhelming them. They should zero in on questions one by one, work them through and seek solutions. The state, the city, and the central school administration should support but not interfere. What is required in schools like these is a set of solutions. There is no justification for keeping the building open simply to observe the state code.

The staff should be kept on during the summer. Give them an air-conditioned retreat; allow them to plan for the year ahead. Work on the program of studies, work on motivation, work on community linkage, work on patterns of staffing, work on everything.

It occurred to me that it might be wise for the boys and girls to be separated —have boys' schools and girls' schools. There are some research data to support this recommendation. I remembered a study in Illinois that I directed a few years ago. There we tried to discover the impact of segregated learning on achievement. We examined a small district where youngsters were feeding into one junior high school out of white schools, black schools, and integrated schools. We were interested in such factors as pupil alienation, attitudes toward schooling, and achievement in the traditional subject fields. We discovered some significant differences, but the overwhelming differences was how boys responded to the learning environments in contrast with how girls responded. The boys were getting the short end of the stick on most things.

Systems should depress the emphasis on attendance. I would even support abandoning compulsory education for this part of the city. Emphasize programs of interest and attractiveness; deemphasize regimentation. Much of the faculty's energy goes into keeping kids in school. And once in school, keeping them in class. Why fight it? Jettison the pressure toward control. Enroll students on the basis of interest only. Such policies violate the rich American tradition of education for everyone, but why carry on the charade? Why?

Again I want it understood that I came away from this school with profound admiration and respect for the regular principal, the three assistant principals, the several counselors, the many teachers, and the many special staff members, as well as the central administration. And I came away with respect for the students. The adults in the building are struggling feverishly. They are dedicated. They are in their own way in love with the school. But they are shell-shocked, exhausted, and desperate. They need help. And I am not sure. I have advanced a few notions but they need careful scrutiny and considerable elaboration.

It is clear that we have no experts in this sort of urban education anywhere. The most expert may be those professionals who are there every day engaging in the fray. But they are reaching out, and it is for this reason that some kind of liaison with universities and other sources of ideas is critical. Refined, umbilical relationsips need to be developed. We are just scratching the surface at Ohio State. No one has the answer. Anyone who thinks he has is a fool. At best there are only partial answers—pieces of a larger mosaic that could at some point in the future fit together in a more productive fashion than today's mosaic.

There are many schools in America like the one I have described. We don't want to admit it but there are. And all of us who bear professional credentials must carry that cross.

Such educational institutions are an indictment of presidents and senators; of justices and teachers; of governors and legislators. It is ludicrous the way we behave. Our pathetic politicians wailing and wringing their hands, spouting platitudes and diatribes. They advance shallow excuses. They say that bold acts will not find favor with unnamed constituencies. And we educators stand impotent, frightened, disheveled in the face of such tragedy.

Problem 2

2–1.   (Individual)

Dean Cunningham is arguing that too much of the unique and valuable contribution of school is destroyed by forcing students who do not want to be there to attend. Would you advocate voluntary high school attendance? Why? Is this point legitimate or merely a cop out?

2–2.   (Individual)

If voluntary attendance were the case, would school be more pleasant and effective? Why?

2–3. (Individual)

If voluntary attendance were the case, would attendance be regular? What would this do to the content presentation plans of teachers?

2–4. (Individual)

If voluntary attendance were the case, what problems would result from larger numbers of unemployed teenagers roaming the streets? Would larger numbers of teenagers be on the streets?

2–5.   (Team Task for Two People)

The current reality, according to Cunningham, is that attendance is irregular now. Discuss with your partner what irregular attendance does to the plans of teachers. Then write a list of methods a teacher can use to assure that students who have been absent can be brought up to date upon their return. Hint: there is no rule saying that the teacher must personally do everything.

2–6.   (Discussion Groups of Four)

Educators talk about teaching the whole child. They design and pursue pedagogical activities. Yet, when sociologists look at schools and at their impact on children they see the impact of the school in a remarkably different light. Whereas an educator would say that school assists the child to develop his potential, a sociologist would say that schools function to eliminate the unworthy from future positions of leadership. What do schools really do? Give examples.

2–7.   (Individual)

Write a brief statement (100 words) of your position on the following issue: Should schools concern themselves with their sociological and psychological impact on children as well as the content they teach?

2–8.   (Individual)

Write a brief statement (100 words) of your current position on the following question:
Should secondary teachers use valuable class time to deal with student concerns not
relating to content? Why?

2–9.   (Position Paper)

Historically, the American school emerged from upper class British tradition and was adapted to the 19th century American condition. This tradition can even be traced as far back as Plato. Many people question the relevance of such a system to students other than advantaged white children. Still others feel that a new system is likely to develop based upon the new realities of the technological age. By the end of this term, prepare a 1000-word paper describing the kind of educational system most likely to exist by 1990. Document your projections where possible. In the concluding paragraphs, draw personal conclusions concerning your own career planning in order to remain up to date during the changes you expect to occur.

Causes of Student Unrest

The following article[3] will add another perspective to the considerations of unrest in American classrooms.

A Federally commissioned study has found that 85 percent of nearly 700 urban high schools recently surveyed had experienced some type of disruptions during the last three years and that racial factors figured in a large number of the incidents.

Dr. Stephen K. Bailey, Chairman of the Policy Institute of the Syracuse University Research Corporation, which made the study for the United States Office of Education, said that "a widespread and volatile situation" existed in the nation's urban secondary schools.

Dr. Bailey, describing the report as an "unsettling story of an unsettling reality," warned that the number and intensity of disruptions would "continue to increase unless met head-on with some imaginative programs."

Findings of the Study

Among the findings of the study, made public yesterday, were the following:

Racially integrated schools are more likely to experience disruptions than those that are almost all white or all black. (The report emphasized, however, that it was not urging segregation as a solution to the problem of disruption.)

Integrated schools with high percentages of black students are less likely to be disrupted if these schools also have high percentages of black staff members. In those schools where the percentage of black students exceeds the percentage of black staff members, disruptions are not only more numerous but take on a more racial tone.

The traditional punitive ways of dealing with student school disruptions—suspension, expulsion, police arrest, in-school detention and referral to parental discipline—often produce "perverse and countraproductive results."

---

[3]Leonard Burder, "Unrest in Urban Schools Linked to Race by Study," *The New York Times* (October 4, 1970). © by the New York Times Company. Reprinted by permission.

The Syracuse report's conclusion that "disruption is positively related to integration" appeared to be in conflict with the findings of another study, also financed by the Office of Education, that was made public last month by the Center for Research and Education in American Liberties at Teachers College, Columbia University.

The center's report, based on a study of the attitudes of 7,000 students attending urban and suburban junior and senior high schools in Greater New York and Philadelphia, suggested that most of the tensions and conflicts were over issues of school governance and individual rights.

However, other studies on school disruption have pointed to race as an important factor.

Last February in Washington, a House subcommittee on general education released the findings of a survey based on responses from more than half of the nation's 29,000 public, private and parochial high schools. Eighteen per cent of the schools reported they had experienced "serious protests" during 1968–69. Racial issues were factors in more than 50 per cent of the protests in schools with more than 1,000 students and in 30 per cent of the smaller schools. The 130-page Syracuse report dealt extensively with the causes of disruption, both in school and in society at large, observing: "The causes of high school disruption run on a circular continuum from the wider society on through the school, and back to the wider society."

Violence Held a Cause

The causes cited ranged from "violence in America" and growing expression of racial and ethnic pride among "America's most oppressed minorities" to lack of student involvement in school policy-making and "cross-cultural clashes" between white and black students and between older white teachers and black students in schools that have changed ethnic character.

The report also suggested some "strategies" for coping with disruption based on apparently successful programs and practices at some schools. These range from the introduction of more flexible educational programs to the use of paid "community aides" as school security personnel.

An official of the Policy Institute in Syracuse, who did not want to be identified, said that the Syracuse report went beyond earlier studies of school disruption by its "comprehensive and candid" treatment of causes and its attention to strategies.

The Syracuse study was requested last spring by Dr. James E. Allen, Jr., before he left the post of United States Commissioner of Education.

The completed report, based on interviews and observations by field research teams sent to 27 high schools in 19 cities (not including New York City) and responses to a detailed questionnaire by principals of 683 urban high schools, was submitted recently. There has so far been no public comment on it from Washington officials.

Disuption Is Defined

Dr. Bailey, who directed the project, is Maxwell Professor of Political Science and former dean of the Maxwell Graduate School of Citizenship and Public Affairs at Syracuse University. He is also a member of the New York Board of Regents, the state's highest education policy-making body.

The Syracuse report defined, for its purpose, a school disruption as "any event which significantly interrupts the education of students." By that it meant strikes or boycotts by teachers or students; property damage, including arson and vandalism; rioting and fighting; physical confrontations between students and staff; picketing and parading; the presence on campus of unruly, unauthorized non-school persons, and "that catch-all phrase—abnormal unruliness among students."

In connection with the study's finding that disruption was more likely to occur in an integrated school, the report declared: "This might suggest a policy of apartheid as a solution to disruption, but this option is unavailable. Among other drawbacks, it is unconstitutional. . . .

"A society polarized between white and black would be almost impossible to manage without even raising the moral stature of the nation as a question. A segregated educational system would hardly train the young for an integrated future when they become adults."

Refuses to Blame Schools

A Syracuse researcher, commenting on the finding that disruption and integration were linked, said: "The troubles in urban high schools these days are often racial—fights between white and black students, the demonstrations and protests that arise from minority groups feeling that some school practices or perhaps some members of the school administration or faculty are racist—so they would naturally be more pronounced in those schools where you have a mixed student body."

Going into the causes of disruption, the report asserted that it would be equally absurd "to lay all the blame for disruption on the schools" or to contend, as have "a few very defensive schoolmen, that a school is 'merely a receptacle for problems it does not create and cannot be responsible for'."

The report pointed to many contributing causes, among them the success of civil rights protests; the effects of slum life; the impact of minority-group pressures on traditionally middle-class oriented public schools; and "the ripple effect on high schools of repeated college and university disruption."

The study's field researchers also found evidence at some schools they visited of a factor that the report calls "black revenge."

"It may be an unpleasant subject," the report said, "but no honest observers of the urban high school scene could bypass the phenomenon of black revenge. We found it sad but psychologically understandable when numbers of black high school students told us one way or another that 'It's Whitey's turn to take some heat.' We note that most urban black young people are fully aware of the long and ugly centuries of disgrace in which they and their kind were oppressed purely on the basis of color . . .

"We found that much of the physical fighting, the extortion, the bullying in and around schools had a clear racial basis. This was particularly apparent where the student mix was predominantly but not wholly black."

Causes of disruption inside the schools most often involved dissatisfaction over social codes, including dress and grooming regulations, and policies governing participation in extracurricular activities.

The report said that while the general practice of requiring students to reach a certain grade level before they can take part in athletics and student government activities was based, "at least in the North, on educational motives, non-white students often regard it as a 'racist practice'."

Student demands for a role in school curriculum planning are "rapidly becoming a third major issue," the study found.

In discussing strategies for preventing or minimizing disruptions, the study said that Berkeley High School (West Campus) in California had reported some success with young adult security personnel who came from the same neighborhoods as the students, while Kettering High School in Detroit had used regular policemen who were young, specially trained and well educated.

The report cited special schools set up to help disruptive students, such as New York City's so-called "600" schools for disturbed youngsters.

Also mentioned were efforts to overcome school "bigness" and to reduce "academic rigidities," such as those undertaken at the new John Adams High School in Portland, Ore., which is organized into four sub-schools, called "houses," with 300 students each.

The report called upon educators to make greater efforts to understand and honor cultural differences, to make possible greater student involvement in school matters that concern them.

The project staff expressed the opinion that "all things being relatively equal, it is a wise policy to promote or recruit a black teacher or administrator rather than a white one in a predominantly black school." Two-thirds of the principals who took part in the survey, the report noted, also agreed with this view.

Comment

The problems discussed by Hundt and Cunningham are, as the Syracuse study revealed, more typical than not. Internal tensions, even disruptions, are common in American schools. The odds that a student teacher or first-year professional will face a crisis involving violence during the first weeks of duty are uncomfortably high.

The racial crisis is a major source of difficulty in American schools, but it is not the only source of trouble. There is tension between all sub-groupings of our culture; each group might lash out at any of the other groups. Care must be taken to avoid oversimplifying the situation.

A major cause of this situation is in the school as an institution. American schools are not integrated in any sense of the word. Integration requires that children interact according to ability and interest, not according to artificial racial or social groupings. Even in desegregated schools different groups are often kept segregated within the building by virtue of class assignments.

Problem 3

3–1.   (Individual)

Name three reasons other than the one discussed here that explain the student unrest and violence problems of the schools.

3–2.   (Individual)

Is discipline really a proper part of school operation? Why?

3–3.   (Individual)

If your answer to 3–2 was yes, describe the limits of discipline. Where does repression start? Where does chaos begin? If your answer to 3–2 was *no,* describe how to avoid the problems of violence. Is discipline a symptom or a cause?

3–4.   (Individual)

Goodman recently charged that student unrest could be best described as "prison riots."[4] Does his view seem justified in the data from Hundt, Cunningham, and the Syracuse Study?

---

[4]Paul Goodman, "High School Is Too Much," *Psychology Today* 4, no. 5 (October 1970): 25.

3–5.   (Task Group of Three)

In order to solve problems between groups it is often necessary to find a common ground in the points of view of the parties involved. Your task is to describe the common ground that exists between students, parents, and teachers. *Starting positions of the three groups:* Students sometimes reject all institutional control and the basic right of the institution to control anyone; parents demand strong discipline to the point of hiring security personnel; teachers merely want to teach and do not want to be bothered by all of this. (Note to Instructor: Assign the task groups so that diverse views are represented within each group.)

Ability Grouping—One Element in the Problem

Many northern schools have reached de facto segregation without the conscious planning and intent which is characteristic of de jure segregation typical of the recent past in the South. Many factors are responsible for de facto segregation. Examples are shifting population patterns and voluntary selection of academic or vocational programs. Ability grouping also emerges as a cause. The following article[5] discusses the problem from this author's viewpoint in 1967. Although the article was written for Ohio readers, the facts are similar throughout the nation. At this writing, the practice remains unchanged. Blacks continue to be sorted into lower ability groups and whites into higher ability groups. This results from the fact that sorting is based upon achievement and, in an informal way, motivation. Black students often fall into the lower groups as the result of previous problems in school—and there they remain.

For some time now the law of the land has been clearly aimed at ending segregation, and school districts throughout the country have been under pressure from civil rights groups and courts to desegregate. Ohio educators are in the midst of this problem, because there still exists substantial de facto segregation.

---

[5]Herbert K. Heger, "Ability Grouping—Can It Be Justified?" *Ohio Schools* (March 1967). Reprinted by permission.

Educators in many urban Ohio school districts are preoccupied with the search for acceptable methods of ending de facto segregation. Results of this dramatic change in school policy and procedure will soon become visible in some of Ohio's leading urban districts.

What will the results be? Will desegregation of the schools achieve pupil integration? Can educators look forward to improving community relations as the result of desegregation?

Current ability grouping practices have a direct influence on all of the preceding questions because these practices determine which children mingle and which are kept apart.

The design and intent of ability grouping practices are pure and honorable. By grouping students of similar abilities in the same class sections or in the same reading group, the teacher can individualize instruction so that the educational process can be accelerated for all. In practice, division of students into their respective ability groups tends to parallel their social class status, and social class status just happens to be heavily race oriented.

Ability grouping, therefore, has a side effect of segregating the races almost as effectively as a planned segregation policy. As soon as a significant number of schools desegregate, the most visible result will be internal segregation of each school, classroom by classroom, and reading group by reading group.

Unless educators exercise significant leadership before civil rights groups discover what will seem to them to be a subversion of national policy, community relations are likely to deteriorate rapidly after this accidental segregation is discovered. When this happens, educational leaders must be prepared to justify the continuance of their grouping policies with evidence that can be understood by all citizens or prepare to abandon grouping. This battle will be fought on a district level by parents, teachers, and administrators because it is at the local level that the discriminatory side effects will become visible.

If we educators begin to discuss the desirability of retaining present grouping policies before the pressure groups become enraged over our apparent duplicity, we will be able to earn greater respect and cooperation of our clientele. If we fail to reach a well documented decision on a district by district basis, we can expect to be inundated in a flood of protests and misunderstandings. Therefore educators in each local school district must consider whether ability grouping should be retained in spite of its incompatability with integration so that the local educators can arrive at an educationally sound decision in time to avoid needless conflict.

In order to support the retention of ability grouping practices, local school districts must show that there are tangible educational advantages which offset the undesirable side effect of segregation. Proponents of ability grouping claim improvement in educational achievement through grouping. They assert that the student can be assigned to a group which closely matches his abilities. The teacher, knowing all students in a certain section are of similar ability, can plan lessons with maximum efficiency and individualization. The central point is that the teacher should alter lessons for each group in order to give all students a chance to learn at their most efficient level and rate.

Unfortunately, research has shown no significant increase in achievement when grouping is used. In addition, some researchers have found that grouping does not significantly reduce the range of abilities in each section. Weaknesses in scheduling and testing procedure tend to nullify the effect of grouping. Many teachers have had experience with misplaced students who were assigned without regard to regular grouping procedure because they had to attend band practice, Spanish IV, or some other special course which is given at just one time. Other teachers are familiar with situations where grouping assignments are made on the basis of insufficient criteria so that students are grouped in all of their subjects according to their ability in only one subject. Such weaknesses persist despite years of intense efforts by educators to improve procedures.

Other researchers have found that teachers do not vary their lesson plans from group to group, or, even worse, they place maximum effort on their favorite high ability groups while unconsciously slacking off on their less favored sections. The effect of such variation of effort is most visible to students in the elementary reading groups where the Bluebirds frequently receive more attention than the Sparrows or Vultures.

Perhaps the most important weakness of grouping is the lack of consideration of a critically important factor in the education of each child. Carl C. Kelley has written in the NEA publication, *Prevention of Failure,* that "How a person feels is more important than what he knows. This is true because one's feelings and attitudes control behavior while one's knowledge does not." That is, knowledge is the tool which provides the means to accomplish goals which are largely determined by a person's feelings and attitudes. Therefore, any successful grouping policy must include consideration of the proper development of feelings and attitudes as well as the mere acquisition of knowledge.

Current grouping practice not only ignores positive development of feelings and attitudes, but has the unfortunate side effect of developing negative feelings and attitudes. Whether a student is in the "slow" section of high school social studies instead of the "college prep" section or is in the "Vultures" reading group instead of the "Bluebirds," he knows that his status is distinctly inferior. He knows he is expected to be unable to do as much as the rest of the students because he has been formally labeled unable, so why should he try?

He also knows that members of his group are less acceptable socially than members of the top group. If the student has the additional burden of a socially unacceptable home, his low group assignment helps reinforce his feeling of rejection and inferiority. This process can result in the division of a school into hostile camps, although more frequently the students at the lower end of the grouping hierarchy simply withdraw into individual shells until they can legally escape their problem by dropping out of school. Such students have negative feelings and attitudes toward their school experience and all of society as the end product of their education. These are the children who will be the problem adults in our society.

This writer is not suggesting that grouping is responsible for all school dropouts and all of the other problems of the slower student. After all, a student can have an equally miserable experience in a randomly-grouped learning situation if the atmosphere is sufficiently hostile. The point is, simply, that one of the duties of educators is to assist the whole child in reaching his maximum potential and that this is not being done under current grouping practice. The coming public controversy over grouping will be racially oriented, but it must be emphasized that current grouping practice falls short of the mark for children of all races and backgrounds.

Mere abandonment of current grouping practice would not automatically correct the shortcomings of the system and certainly would not prevent criticism of the school's failure to successfully carry out the spirit of integration.

What is needed is a carefully thought-out program of student assignment to class sections which would assure the proper atmosphere for the positive development of attitudes and feelings which are so important to the success of a democratic society. This program should provide a system of class assignment which will assure that each class section will be socially balanced with boys and girls of all socio-economic backgrounds, all religions, and all races found in the school district.

Only under such a system of "social grouping" can students have sufficient personal contact with students from other backgrounds to learn that other people are not so very different and thereby develop attitudes and feelings suitable for citizens of a democracy. In addition, such a plan can go a long way toward eliminating the self image of mediocrity which students in slower groups now have. Such a plan can expand the students' horizons, assist the development of a more accurate, realistic view of society and people, and can aid in dispelling many myths held by children from narrow backgrounds. Naturally, the design and implementation of any plan to improve grouping practice requires local action by individual school districts in order to assure that widely varying local needs are met.

The district which adopts a practice to enhance the development of democratic feelings and attitudes will win the respect of its community and will avoid any crisis over grouping practice. Other school districts will be faced by a new series of controversies over the issue of ability grouping.

The intensity of these controversies will depend on how well current practices meet the needs of the local community. It is certain, however, that any multi-racial school district which decides to retain ability grouping must somehow correct the major faults of the system or be prepared to weather a major storm of criticism.

Problem 4

4–1. (Individual)

Which is more important to you: grouping people by ability for purely instructional goals or grouping students for social rather than instructional objectives?

4–2. (Discussion)

Federal Judge Skelly Wright, less than a year after the publication of the preceeding article, ordered the District of Columbia to abandon its ability grouping practices for the reasons described in the article. At the time this book was being written, the Department of Health, Education and Welfare was pursuing the new standard that ability grouping is unconstitutional if it results in racial segregation. Public policy is still to prevent segregation—not to force integration—yet ability grouping may be eliminated in the school you select to start your career. Will this change help students accept each other as equals? Why? What remains to be done?

4–3.   (Individual)

What problems will teachers face as ability grouping is phased out? Can you see any problems of public acceptance of this concept?

4–4.   (Individual)

How would you cope with this shift in school operation? Hint: would grouping by ability for short periods of time be any better than permanent year-long assignments? Would regular shakeups of group assignments at predetermined intervals of, say, one month help?

4–5.   (Individual)

What impact would the abolition of ability grouping have on *your* teaching style? How would you adjust your lessons to the fast and not-so-fast students?

4–6.   (Task Groups of Four)

In small group work sessions, design alternative grouping approaches that do not discriminate. Try to assure that students can mix on the basis of interests and abilities rather than on social status. Try to consider the possibility of having students work part of the time without teacher presence.

Teaching versus Control in the Urban School

The documentation emerging from the American high school tends to indicate that many, and in some places most, students are in school against their will. There are students who have given up or who were not motivated for success in the first place. These are students who are disadvantaged in terms of preparation for school, ability, or some other reasons. These are students who have "dropped out," are not interested in society, and have no personal goals. Many of these students are in school by virtue of parental pressure or social pressure (truant officer). Many of these students have no better place to go. All of these students desire only a quiet haven in which to socialize. They don't want to work, they don't care about the same things the faculty cares about. They won't play the teacher's game; they are "internal drop-outs."

The tragedy is that most schools have found no solution to the problems involved in motivating and teaching the internal drop-out. The students who refuse to learn become a body to be herded about, a body to control. Control often is accomplished by repression.

The teachers and faculty have no desire to repress; they don't want to run a school that is like a prison. They don't want to have private police on hall duty. They don't want to keep rest rooms locked, except for brief supervised periods. They don't want to keep classroom doors and entrances locked. They just have not been able to figure out alternatives.

What is it like to face the daily problems of the urban school? The following problems address that question.

Problem 5

5–1.   (Individual)

If you taught in the school described by Cunningham, you would face a group of thirty to forty teenagers for forty minutes a day for about 190 days. Absentee rates run rather high, so you would have each child for about 100 hours in a group setting. How can you motivate, teach, and alter the life style of *each* child under those conditions? How can you, in 100 hours out of the life of a child from an impoverished home, change educational trends that were established in elementary school and before?

5–2.   (Individual)

You are a young woman teacher. You have seen two large boys rob small students on two occasions. You order the boys to report to the office but they threaten to harm you in every possible manner and they leave the school building. You discuss this incident with an older teacher and find that these two juveniles have exacted revenge on teachers before and prosecution has failed. What do you do?

5–3.   (Individual)

A bulletin arrives from the central administration together with a set of materials dealing with drug abuse from a drug company. You are *ordered* to teach each child how to detect drug addicts and how to report them. You already know that half of your students are on dope. You sincerely believe that drugs are harmful. What strategy should you use? Describe it below.

Games Teachers Play

Another source of difficulty in American schools is that teachers operate according to rigid, inflexible rituals with little variation, and they don't teach the rituals to the children. Middle- and upper-class children learn how to play school at home but many students never learn how to play the "School Game."

Game theory is very revealing when applied to classrooms. James B. MacDonald presents one view in the following article.[6]

> *The Information-Giving Game.* The most common communication game in our high schools may be called information-giving. This game is exactly what it suggests. The teacher has information which he forms and manages to send to the student receiver. The receivers are expected to take in this information without distorting it and signal the teacher that they have the information. The media by which messages may be sent are variable, but the intent of the process is relatively constant.
>
> The roles assigned are clear. The teacher possesses the information or has knowledge of avenues of access to this information. His role is to present to, or put students in contact with, the ideas or facts in the most effective manner. The student role is also clear. He is to receive the information and be able to show the teacher that he has possession of it.
>
> The rules of the game are less obvious, but derivable by analysis. Some of these are:
>
> 1. The game should be played seriously—all participants are expected to accept the worth and significance of the game and to cooperate and perform in a serious work-like atmosphere.
> 2. The teacher directs the game—students are expected to take their cues for responding from the teacher. The teacher of course is responsible for initiating and soliciting responses.
> 3. Attention and cooperation are expected—students are expected to be attentive and to cooperate with the teacher to achieve the goals of the game.
>
> The goals of the game are also fairly obvious. Students are expected to be able to reproduce the information presented in whatever form the teacher calls for. Their reproductions are graded and become part of the competitive interpersonal data of our society. The goals of the game vary. Some are, for example, to please the teachers, beat fellow students, win access to social mobility, or simply to know something.
>
> Rituals are also involved. Students are expected (usually) to raise their hands before responding. Teachers are expected to have the last word and "cap" any set of responses. People take turns and talk one at a time; and all

---

[6]James B. MacDonald, "Gamesmanship in the Classroom," *National Secondary School Principals Bulletin* 50, no. 314 (December 1966): 51–68.

follow the special procedures for handing in assignments, taking tests, coming and going, and relating to each other.

The language of the game is essentially framed in a question-answer, lecture, and discussion format. Outside the classroom the teacher talks about individual "IQ's," meeting the "needs of students," "gifted," "culturally deprived," and a host of other things. Inside the classroom the special language relates to cueing the smooth working of the process. "Who would like to tell us about Charlemagne?" might be interpreted to mean "All right, let's get started; who is first?" Each teacher has her use of "good," "o.k.," and other phrases that are a distinctive use of language in the communication process.

The values of the game are found in achievement. Excellence means knowing the subject, and excellent teaching means getting the information across. Most often the standard is a comparative one, sometimes an absolute one, and infrequently an individual one.

Mastery. A subvariety of information-giving is the mastery game. In general it follows the same kinds of prescriptions as information-giving. However, the special context of drill and practice provides variation for this game.

The goals, for example, might be thought of as "over-learning" or habitualizing rather than "just" knowing. Many skills fall in this area and the basic intent is to take them into cognition and make them so automatic that cognitive awareness of them is no longer necessary for behavior.

The Problem-Solving Game. The next most common appearance in high school is the problem-solving game. The teacher role is to present, get students in contact with, or evolve a problem with them. The teacher often knows the [proper] or [at least] an answer to this problem, but if not he has knowledge of how to solve it or faith that it can be solved. Oftentimes problem-solving takes place in a project or "activity" format.

The student role is more active than in information-giving. He is now expected to take some initiative, to think about what he is doing as well as what he is learning. The goal of the game is to come up with some satisfactory resolution of the problem, and standards of excellence are applied in terms of the teacher's judgement of the exhaustion of relevant sources of data in relation to the level of maturity of the students.

Rules of the game are built around the expectation that students will define or see a problem and set out systematically and thoughtfully to solve it. Contrary to information-giving, it is now taboo to expect the teachers to provide answers. Language usage now shifts to terms such as "resource materials," "critical thinking," and analysis of the process of reflective thinking with such concepts as inference, data, and evidence becoming part of the setting.

The Discovery or Inquiry Game. The discovery or inquiry game is a variant of problem-solving. The major difference rests in the goals of the game. Each begins with discrepancies to be resolved, but in inquiry the goal is shifted from the solution to the process of solving a problem.

The teacher role is to set the circumstances for discrepant awareness on the part of students. Students are expected to search, manipulate, experiment, and seek actively.

The rituals in this case may often become the modes of inquiry and be in essence the goals. Thus, when appropriate, a student must use the ritual of scientific method, or of formal logic, or of aesthetic criticism, or of moral and ethical evaluation.

The value of the game is in playing, intelligently and with spirit. The outcomes of the game are seen primarily in terms of the process utilized, and excellence becomes awareness of the process of inquiry.

The Dialogue Game. Upon occasion the communication game can actually move to the level of dialogue. In a true dialogue game the roles of all present are the same—the attempt to move the discussion to the revelation of insights not present in any participant at the beginning of the interaction.

The rules of the game are:

1. One participates as a total person, not as a role player.
2. One is expected to be open, to reveal himself, and to receive from and listen to others.
3. One must be disciplined. One is expected to participate and one is expected to participate in the context of the contribution of others.
4. One must respond to others and therefore be responsible in relation to them.

No contributions are rejected, criticized, or judged per se. Participants, however, are expected to discipline themselves by the monitoring of behavior which reflects personal needs to talk, show off, play one-upmanship, defend themselves, or pull rank. The goal is to explore beyond the present member-awareness for insights and implications about the material which produces an aesthetic reponse or an insight (Aha!).

Further, the goal is to relate the forms of content or subject matters to the vitality which originally produced them; to bring the meanings that come out of a student's living into conjunction with the meanings inherent in the subject matter. Excellence is assured by the feeling of time well spent and the satisfaction of new awarenesses.

Ritual and language will be loosened and, although the spatial arrangements of facilities for dialogue may reflect circular rather than linear patterns, time may be used more flexibly; and the use of judgmental terms will be negated.

The Clarification Game. Attempts to relate students to meanings and values are often found in clarification procedures. The teacher, in other words, attempts to elicit personal responses, reactions, and meanings to life and subject matter. The teacher's role is to focus the student inward and the student's role is to express attitude feelings, aspirations, values, and impressions and to reflect upon them.

The rules of the game are very open. The teacher must never judge any student response; he must never ask questions for which he has a predetermined answer but only questions for which an individual student could possibly have the answer. Students, on the other hand, must freely express their real feelings, concerns and meanings.

The goal of clarification is the development of values and commitments in the form of personal meanings attached to content. Standards of excellence are difficult to express, but if the process is satisfying the worth is assumed.

The language involves such phrases as "tell me more about that" or "now I see what you're saying," or "you mean to say . . .?" All language involves "I feel," "I think," and other first-person reference. Again, ritual is caught in the use of time and space of a personal and flexible nature.

Problem 6

6–1.   (Discussion Groups of Six)

Does the system with its grading, grouping, pass-fail rituals encourage teachers to play games with children? How? List the specific ways that such games affect children.

6–2. (Individual)

What happens as children participate in the school game without knowing the rules?

6–3. (Individual)

Assume the children cannot play one of MacDonald's games but they are subjected to the game for years at a time. Would they create their own *"survival game"*? Describe a game a student might play based on a withdrawal strategy.

6–4.   (Individual)

Suppose the student in the previous problem becomes hostile in his agony. What kind of survival game might he play?

6–5.   (Individual)

Teachers tend to play certain games in the classroom. Children from the inner city do not know how to play these games. Propose a solution.

6–6.   (Task Teams of Two)

Design a lesson structure so that inner city children can play the "teacher's game" in the classroom.

The Tale of Peter and the Rabbit

Organization, discipline, and control are not the only problems in the urban school. Perhaps one of the most serious problems arises from the radically different experiential background of the teachers and of the students.

Teachers, whether black or white, are usually middle class, have had some travel experience, and have seen a sample of the "finer" things of life. Perhaps more important is the fact that they do not understand how living in a slum alters a person's outlook on life, and they often fail to understand how hard it is for children to visualize something beyond their experience.

Ghetto children, whether from a Spanish or black ghetto or a poor white slum, have not been exposed to the same range of experiences as their teachers. Many have not seen rabbits, cows, or corn. Some do not really understand modern technical devices, nor do they care.

Teachers and ghetto children often find it very hard even to talk to each other because their frames of reference are so different. Witness the following episode.[7]

"Class, look at this picture, and tell me what you see," said the teacher.

Hands went up, but the teacher called on Peter, whose hand had not been one of them. "Peter, what is it?"

"It looks like a rat."

The class laughed. Someone said, "Peter is so stupid. He doesn't know a rat from a rabbit."

The teacher said, "Peter, what's the matter with your eyes? Can't you see that it has long ears?"

"Yes," said Peter weakly.

"It is a rabbit, isn't it Peter?"

"Yes," he said.

"Today's story is about a rabbit," said the teacher, pointing to the picture and then the word. "It's a story about a hungry white rabbit. What do you suppose a rabbit eats when he's hungry?"

"Lettuce," said Mary.

"Carrots," said Suzy.

"Meat," said Peter.

The class laughed. Someone said, "Peter is so stupid. He doesn't know what rabbits eat."

"Peter, you know very well that rabbits don't eat meat," said the teacher.

"That depends on how hungry they are," said Peter. "When I'm hungry, I'll eat anything my mother gives me, even when I don't like it."

"Don't argue, Peter," said the teacher. "Now, Class, how does a rabbit's fur feel when you pet him?" asked the teacher.

"Soft," said Suzy.

"Silky," said Mary.

---

[7]Eugene Grant, "Peter and the Rabbit," *Phi Delta Kappan* 49 (November 1967). Reprinted by permission.

"I don't know," said Peter.

"Why?" asked the teacher.

"Cause I wouldn't pet one. He might bite me and make me sick, like what happened to my little brother, the time a hungry one got on his bed when he was sleeping."

The class laughed. Someone said, "Peter is fibbing. He knows his mother doesn't allow rabbits in bed."

After the class had read the story and had their recess, the teacher said to the supervisor, "I hate to sound prejudiced, but I'm not sure that this busing from one neighborhood to the other is good for the children."

The supervisor shook his head sadly and said to the teacher, "Your lesson lacked one very important ingredient."

"What was that?" asked the teacher.

"A rabbit," said the supervisor.

Problem 7

7–1. (Individual)

What kind of student is Peter?

7–2. (Individual)

What kind of students comprise the rest of the class?

7–3. (Individual)

What is the background of the teacher?

7–4. (Individual)

What animal is Peter talking about?

7–5. (Discussion Groups of Six)

Is Peter's information about rats correct? Can rats really be as large as rabbits? Record group opinion.

7–6. (Discussion Groups of Six)

How does this affect Peter's interest in animals and in stories about animals? Record group opinion.

7–7. (Discussion of Groups of Six)

Peter sees things differently from the other children. What effect does this have on teaching strategy?

7–8.   (Individual)

You hate rats and you don't want to hear about the slums Peter lives in. How do you maintain empathy for Peter? How do you teach him?

7–9.   (Individual)

Peter is an elementary child. How will he act by the time he reaches junior high school if he is continually exposed to experiences like this?

7–10.   (Task Groups of Three)

You are a seventh grade teacher and Peter has arrived in your class. He has undergone many experiences like the one you have been considering. Based on your answer to the previous problem, what can you do to re-interest him in school? How long will it take to reestablish motivation to participate and learn? Report a solution an individual teacher can use.

A Critical Incident in Teacher Adjustment

The problems treated to this point should establish a clear basis for understanding why so many teachers leave the profession. Cunningham and Hundt have made clear that most beginning teachers face serious adjustment problems as they assume the practitioner's role. The person facing the most severe problems is often the quiet student in the back of the education class.

Occasionally one of the quiet ones breaks his silence and provides us with an insight into the problems that may be representative of his group. An example of such a breach in the wall of silence was provided by a student in one of the author's education courses. This student turned an ordinary critique of Liebow's *Tally's Corner*[8] into a plea for help in resolving his personal racial crisis. This bright young man was suffering from a conflict in values which his intellectual skills and open-mindedness had not been able to overcome. With a great show of courage he suppressed his concern for a good grade and for social acceptance and bared his soul for inspection. The results are a powerful picture of inner conflict that may be typical of many teacher candidates.

How can the white middle-class teacher candidate resolve his inner conflicts which are the result of the clash between his heritage, the events of the day, and the pronouncements of his professors?

Following his paper the responses of three educators to the issues raised by this student are presented.

Tally's Corner upset me. Like everyone else in America I've thought about race a good deal recently. My parents have mixed ideas on the subject: my father has a romantic love for the Old South, a long family tradition of conservative Republicanism, coupled with a warm feeling for colored people whom he feels work for their living, while my mother has an occasionally stated belief that most Negroes are inferior to white people, along side of a real sympathy for those in need. Involved in our family racial attitudes is the role of Mary, a colored woman who has worked for us for thirty-four years. She and my mother have spent many hours together, and she helped raise my brother and me. All of us love her. We also have a part-time maid who has worked for us for several years. She is a deeply Christian, hard working woman we all like. When I was in high school I strongly supported the civil rights movement, thinking that it would help out Mary's people. When I went to Virginia my freshman year in college my parents warned me not to be too radical. I, nevertheless, stayed sympathetic to civil rights during my college years although my love for the past, especially the Old South, also grew. These two feelings were not compatible, needless to say, but I kept them both until I graduated from Denison. After that I went to Columbia for a year and participated in the first Harlem school boycott. This experience frightened me; Negro children were taught to sing the "Negro National Anthem" and given literature to read that was intensely hostile to the South. New York

---

[8]Elliot Liebow, *Tally's Corner* (Boston: Little, Brown and Company), 1967.

itself depressed me with its vomiting drunks, its pushy subway crowds, its endless ugliness. But I knew New York was modern America, the rest of the country becoming more like it every day. One April morning I went to Princeton. The train went through the north Jersey factories and slag heaps, then came to Princeton where the tulip trees were blooming in the Gothic quadrangles and the boys had good manners. I suddenly gave up the twentieth century. Even if this Princeton world was *mock*-medieval, *phony* dignified, I liked it better. The next week I went to Charlottsville to interview at the University of Virginia, and I found my new home. Here was a place almost free of the twentieth century. When I walked on a warm night under the long colonnade built by Thomas Jefferson I could almost hear the soft voices of the planters' sons who made The University the leading school in the South before the War Between the States.

I lived there for two years, happily surrounded by those beautiful green hills, far from strikes and riot.

This fall I'm going to teach in South Carolina because I think more of the best of the Old South is preserved there than anywhere else. I'll be living in a small conservative community, and I hope I'll be accepted there as a fellow citizen.

I imagine all this disgusts you, Mr. Heger, but I don't want to offend you because I've learned to like and admire you. Still I had to say it to explain my reaction to *Tally's Corner.* I still love Mary and I still feel every human being has the right to decent food and shelter, but I no longer support the civil rights movement of the moderate period, and I violently reject the new movement of Black Power.

I tried, in spite of all this, to read *Tally's Corner* as open mindedly as possible. It was interesting to see how those colored men lived their lives day by day, and I was slightly surprised to see how much they are like college men in their exploitive attitudes towards women and their emphasis on friendships which usually are close but not lasting. And I can even partially accept Liebow's justification of them on the grounds that they are defeated before they begin by economic forces that only allow them to hold low paying jobs they know won't lead anywhere. But all the way through the book I kept feeling this is one-sided, this is a piece designed to support a position the author is already committed to. Of course each book reflects its author's basic views but, knowing this, do I have to accept his views, because he has marshalled some evidence for them? No, I say—I can marshal some evidence for mine too. If, as Liebow implies, Tally and Sea Cat and the others are the fathers of numerous illegitimate children, seldom work, and frequently get into trouble with the police because of their environment, then why are some Negroes who have had a similar environment better? Even Liebow says on page 139 that one of the women in the Carry Out area has a government job where she never misses a day's work. What made her different? Couldn't it be what many have said all along—individual initiative and better heredity? And isn't it possible that the average level of achievement of Negroes is lower than that of whites because they are, as a group, less gifted in certain things than we are? Why, after all, has Africa, alone of the continents, never produced a high native civilization? I don't know the answers to these questions and right now I think no one can, but until the liberals' evidence is overwhelming, I choose to accept the orderly dignity of the Old South rather than the anarchy of the present, Robert E. Lee rather than Stokely Carmichael.

Problem 8

8–1.   (Discussion Groups of Five)

Among white teacher candidates, how typical are these feelings?

8–2.   (Discussion Groups of Five)

As a person with the convictions of this teacher teaches, what kind of impact will he have on his students, white or black? Describe the impact.

8–3.   (Discussion Groups of Five)

Can a teacher who feels as this young man overcome his inner self in teaching? Can he teach what is "right" rather than what he feels?

8–4.   (Individual)

Write an individual reaction to the problem discussed under 8–3.

The Author's Response to this Student

It is not possible to withdraw from the problems of society. Those people who choose to live in a world of isolation from the problems of race will inevitably find their dream world rudely shattered by the winds of change. If this student retreats from the problems of race, he is resigning himself to the role of a victim of events and he will suffer the fate of such victims: bitterness, despair, and intellectual death. The most important point that this student needs to understand is that he needs to take some positive, creative role, no matter how small, which will lead to improvement in the human condition. It is not necessary for everyone to be a leader in the search for solutions to the racial question, but some involvement is absolutely necessary in order for our young student to maintain a sense of *control* over his own fate and in order to protect his own self-concept.

What kinds of involvement are best for this young man? Clearly he is not cut out to be a civil rights leader, and on the basis of his performance in my class and after a personal conference with him I would say that he is making a wise professional choice. He is likely to be a fine college instructor in his discipline. His professional goal of teaching in a small southern college seems appropriate.

This young man should begin by improving his general education. There are several major factual errors in his argument, errors which are commonly accepted and which seem logical. He needs to improve his factual knowledge of the racial problem. He has lumped at least five kinds of problems under race: racial, social, economic, historic, and psychological. The first task is to investigate these separate aspects of poverty. He will be surprised to find how many of the problems of motivation and achievement are in no way racial. He needs to compare the rural Negro to the lowland white sharecropper and to the mountaineer; he needs to compare the urban Negro to the Puerto Rican and the lower-class urban white.

Once equipped with more accurate facts about the true nature of the problems of race and poverty, our student will be better able to analyze his own outlook on society. If he never does any more than learn the real facts and convey them to his Southern students, he will be providing a significant kind of leadership in breaking the Negro myth.

Another aspect of this young man's feelings which deserves attention is his revulsion for the urban situation. This writer thoroughly shares his feelings, and wonders whether megalopolis is a fit place for any man, rich or poor. But the urban way is a fact of life. We all live *with* it, and most of us *in* it. This student somehow feels that the North is urban and the South is rural and never the twain shall meet. But the South is no longer much different from the North; it is becoming more urbanized all of the time. If this student wants to retreat to a small college town and live the quiet life that should be his privilege, but he owes it to his students to visit and study megalopolis and to prepare his students to meet the urban challenge for *they will surely live in the city.*

The recommendations made here may seem superficial. Perhaps so, but they are a start toward a solution of the problem. This student has felt the need to retreat even before he has seen the problem in all of its massive ugliness. In totality the problem does seem hopeless, but when taken in small portions the task becomes manageable.

Our student tried eating his entire steak in one bite; now he must learn to cut the steak into bite-sized pieces.

Problem 8 (continued)

8–5.   (Teams of Two)

What separate factors are involved in this student teacher's problem?

8–6.   (Teams of Two)

What factual errors did this anonymous student make in his concluding paragraph?

8-7.   (Teams of Two)

How should this person and other teacher candidates respond to this personal value problem?

A Black Educator's Response

A second response to the problems of the anonymous student by Dr. Jean Emmons, a black educator, "From the Other Side of the Fence," adds another perspective to the issue.

It has been said that "originality does not consist in saying what no one has ever said before, but in saying exactly what you think yourself." I hold this philosophy and I shall endeavor to say in my own way.

This paper is an attempt to condense into a few pages some thoughts concerning the development of some paths of understanding about the American poor, focusing on the Negro American. The limitations of space prevent discussing the Puerto Rican American, the Spanish American, the Chinese American, the Japanese American, the Indian American, and last but not least the Appalachian American and other American poor.

I hope these paths will serve as first steps in helping the advantaged understand the urban poor and why many of them came to be that way. Further, it is hoped that the advantaged will use these understandings to recognize differences, why they exist, the good that has come to our country because of these differences, and the necessity for differences to continue to exist if this country is to fulfill the promise of leadership. Then and only then will the advantaged be able to reach across (not down) with a helping hand to those we classify as disadvantaged. We must see that the door to continued opportunity remains open to all persons in all styles of life, and this door must remain open in a manner conducive to the internal development of those who elect to pass through it. The advantaged must remain ready to keep the doors of opportunity open. This is a delicate task. Yet through this achievement both the disadvantaged and the advantaged will take pride in their heritage and the development of a rich mixture of "fluid-difference" will be promoted.

The Urban Poor. The urban poor and their problems represent an area of national urgency today. Our educational concern had paused to focus on the "culturally disadvantaged," "children who come to school with less" or whatever euphemism one chooses.

We shall focus here on the Negro child in the inner-city since, as previously stated, it would be very difficult within the confines of one short paper to include the other ethnic urban poor groups.

Historical Background of the Urban Negro Poor. In reviewing some possible causes of recent rioting by the Negro in the large metropolitan area Moynihan states "... first and foremost is unemployment. The Depression has never ended for the slum Negro."[9]

Why is this true? Why has the Negro, more than any other ethnic group migrating to large Northern cities, been subjected constantly to low (if any) wages, miserable housing, and racial discrimination?

It could reasonably be said that just about every urban ethnic minority has suffered from class segregation at one time or another in America as evidenced by the historical development of America's big cities. As one reviews history, one sees an emerging pattern of movement from in to out as defined as into the inner-city and then from the inner-city to outer-city suburbia. The process was the "system's" way of acculturating its immigrant groups and it somehow seemed to provide release to the next sector in keeping with the indigent's education, training, wants, needs, wishes, desires, ability and/or luck, to move from his present station of life.

This process was facilitated by successive immigrant groups that needed or desired acculturation to the "American Way"; thus the "system" worked smoothly and successfully for approximately one hundred years.

About the time of World War I systematic factors set upon this nation to bring this process to a halt.

These factors can be identified as:

1. The development of the mass production system
2. The movement of America from the observer of innovations to the creator of and user of innovations
3. The movement of America from an importing, consuming nation to a producing, exporting nation
4. The movement of America's consumers from a cash to a debt basis

---

[9]Daniel Moynihan, "Liberals, the 'Under Class' and '67 Riots—a Critical Review," *The Catholic Times* (August 27, 1967).

5. The continued development in America of sophisticated mass transportation systems (passenger railroads, freight railroads, inter-urban
   railroads, and intra-urban railroads)
6. The development in America of the most elaborate communication
   system the world had ever seen at that time (the newspapers, tele-
   graph, and the beginnings of the telephone)
7. The production needs of a massive global war
8. The development of a massive educational system.

These things and many more created a seemingly insatiable need for additional labor. America, possessing the inventive, creative and constructive
genius it had continually shown to that point in its development, immediately
tapped the largest, strongest, most productive, closest and the least abrasive
labor force that was available—the Southern Negro. Therefore, this new force
was coaxed, courted, persuaded, induced, even kidnapped to the large Northern cities to perform the work so sorely needed. He became the "last of the
Mohicans"—the last immigrant.

Today, approximately fifty years later, the American Negro has found, to
his dismay, the bitter experience of being last. This coupled with the fact that
his country has never been able to accept him as being within the parameters
of all the great American doctrines, has re-made him a slave, an "in-colonial."

We now view him at the end of the historically significant fifty year "lock-
in." He has been "locked-in" because no other group came to take his place.[10]
He has been "locked-in" because of skin color and thus high visability. He
has been "locked-in" as a victim of racial mythology propagated by the racist
whites—so strongly that he came to believe it himself. He believed that he was
different, that his was a "racial" (and thus permanent and fixed) difference
rather than an "ethnic" difference. This difference then was interpreted by
whites and Negroes as inferior.

Thus inner-city has become the birthplace and the burial ground of the
American Negro.

In a 1965 U.S. Department of Labor study,[11] the statement was made:
"There is absolutely no question of any genetic differential: Intelligence potential is distributed among Negro infants in the same proportion and pattern
as among Icelanders or Chinese or any other group. American society, however, impairs the Negro potential."

In spite of this and other studies supporting the notion that Negro children
are *not* inherently inferior intellectually, Moynihan reports: "For five years
or more, we have known that Negro children were doing very badly even in
schools that would have to be described as quite good. For some time we have
known that the net results, the failure rate on Selective Service examinations,

---

[10]This is true in spite of Chicanos and Puerto Ricans and other minority groups who now work in the
service industry, at jobs formerly defined as "Negro" jobs.

[11]"The Negro Family," Office of Policy Planning and Research, Washington, D.C., U.S. Department of
Labor (March 1965), p. 78.

were near horrendous until recently; something like 56% of Negro youth called up for the draft have been failing the mental test—a sixth grade examination."[12]

The U.S. Report [1965 Department of Labor study] clearly states that people tend to be born equal and similar in terms of their mental characteristics. The Moynihan report clearly states that this American called the Negro ends up eighteen years later vastly different from his white counterpart in mental characteristics. This is evidenced in part by his performance on the Selective Service Mental Test. May we then ask why? What has happened? When did it happen? Why did it happen? Who was responsible? And finally, the most searching question of all—could it have been prevented?

In light of the findings of the kinds of research cited above, programs of every sort have been and are being provided *for* the poor and *to* the poor, *for* the schools and *to* the schools. Some of these programs are meeting with varying degrees of success in terms of their stated objectives. A number are not. James Olsen states what he believes to be the cause for less than desired success of these programs in many instances: "They emphasize the environmental limitations of the slum and the bad effects of those limitations on learning. The fact is that we are building our educational programs almost exclusively around the weaknesses and defects of low-income people."[13]

In all fairness, it seems that we must be aware of some shifts in this attitude of a few years back. We are becoming educated to the notion that the American Negro desires not that action be undertaken *to* and *for* him but rather that OPPORTUNITY, primarily in the form of JOB OPPORTUNITY, be afforded to him. When this is accomplished, he will be in a position to undertake his own action. Further, it seems we are becoming increasingly aware of the fallacy of the notion that inner-city poor children are not socialized. These children *are* indeed socialized, though socialized in ways that are admittedly quite different from those of the middle-class advantaged child. Could this be the crux of the problem? The inner-city poor child doesn't necessarily come to school with quantitatively "less," he *may*, in fact, come with "more"—but "more" of those kinds of experiences and attitudes which baffle our middle-class consciousness and thus render our middle-class teachers helpless.

Haro Öostdyk, who is a white man, conducting what he terms "street academics"—in a black environment—in Harlem for the purpose of preparing high school dropouts for college, states this in more colorful terms:

"You've got to know a lot to survive on these streets. These kids know how the numbers game works, what cop is on the take from whom. Suffering and struggle has hurt a great foundation in these kids. They have a language, very expressive and colorful. The school system says forget all that nasty stuff and

---

[12]Daniel Moynihan, "Liberals, the 'Under Class' and the '67 Riots—A Critical Review," *The Catholic Times* (August 27, 1967).

[13]James Olsen, "Challenge of the Poor to the Schools," *Phi Delta Kappan* 47, no. 2 (October 1965), pp. 79–84.

don't use your language. Put all that out of your head and let us fill it with something else. The kids won't do it. But if you respect what they know you can help them to build other knowledge on that."[14]

The argument in certain aspects holds true for all minorities, for all poor, for all disadvantaged.

Our 19th century system has not been updated sufficiently to accomodate the needs of our 20th century sophistication. This we must do. We must reconstruct substantial parts of our massive educational system, for it is the system that must bear the twofold burden of society—maintenance and progression. It is in the latter area that we have not taken cognizance of the new viability of our total system. We must therefore address ourselves to the delicate task of improving upon that which we have so sturdily maintained. Or perhaps as one of my colleagues has argued repeatedly, the maintenance function has lost its usefulness. We need massive overhauling to the extent that a new system must be created. This new system will have built-in substantive mechanism for automated change geared to needs of the sub-system and geared also to the needs of the total system. This system will be highly sensitive and articulate. It can be envisioned as helping the 21st century citizen develop himself into an entity that is capable of socio-economic and political understandings such that would prevent him from falling into the erroneous thinking that all who are different from him are bad and should therefore be destroyed (or at least severely contained).

In conclusion, I would staunchly defend the right of any American to choose the life style most comfortable to him. But, to have the ability to choose suggests that a certain level of knowledge exists and also more important that a certain guarantee exists—that every man not only have that right to choose but that he must also have the alternative available.

---

[14]Roger Boardwood, "The New Negro Mood," *Fortune* (January 1968), pp. 146–51.

Problem 8 (continued)

8–8.   (Individual)

Emmons suggests that inner-city children come to school with more socialization than teachers suspect. In fact there are areas in which young teachers are more naive than slum children. Can you name some such areas?

8–9.   (Individual)

The "maintenance function" is to preserve social values and pass them to the next generation. Emmons suggests that the maintenance function may have lost its purpose in American schools. Describe what Emmons implies as a substitute for this function.

8–10.   (Presentation Problem, Task Groups of Six)

The problem under discussion is psychological as well as conceptual. In what ways can a beginning teacher cope with the psychological stress? What impact does the data presented by Dr. Emmons have on your perceptions of a successful strategy for coping with your personal adjustment problems? Discuss your answers in groups and present your class with a summation of strategies.

8–11.   (Discussion Groups of Six)

Spokesmen for minority groups have often said that equality for minorities is not enough. In many respects we, as a nation, have achieved official equality, yet real progress in assisting minorities to participate equally has not been made. Our nation is looking to the schools for the solution. Discuss what the schools can do to help minorities to achieve true equality. Perhaps an illustration can assist your discussion. If an amateur enters a boxing ring to compete with a professional boxer, one can say that they will compete equally as far as the rules of the game are concerned. After three rounds of being badly beaten by the professional, the amateur still enters the fourth round on an equal basis with the professional. (The American black is comparable to the fourth round amateur.) The problem is that although round four may be equal, it is clearly not equitable. How can the match be made equitable?

The Third Educator Speaks

Another response to the problems of the anonymous teacher has been made by Dr. Paul Klohr in "The Larger Question."

This young teacher's candid recognition of the dilemma he faces with respect to his feelings about race and civil rights is a moving illustration of the value conflicts so many of us now confront in the American scene. And since his account of his life leads one to believe that he is fundamentally concerned about human values, it is predictable that he will continue to face this conflict *within himself.* Such will be the case in spite of the temporary reprieve he assumes he has found in South Carolina.

The consequences of this kind of inner conflict for an individual can be tragic, indeed, if he cannot find healthy ways to cope with it. Suppressed guilt feelings, authoritarian thinking, over-simplistic solutions, increased alienation—not to mention ulcers—tend to be some of the widespread consequences. But even more critical in the long haul is the strong possibility that this young man will become less human than he might otherwise be. And, being less than fully human, himself, he cannot bring all of his potential resources into his work as a *teacher.* In effect, he and many others are caught up in a dehumanizing society.

We are increasingly being dehumanized in that we do not have access to help as we attempt to address ourselves directly to the kinds of value-laden dilemmas this man faces. There is glib talk about the need to carry on "dialogues" with one another and to create more effective social arrangements —including institutions that respond to human needs. But it is a rare school or university that fulfills this role, and churches, for the most part, lack relevancy. Where, then, does our new industrial state, with its technological model of man—and its mishmash of unexamined values such as, for example, the stereotypes of the so-called "Protestant Ethic" and the "left-wing" civil rights worker which seem so pervasive in this young man's analysis of his own feelings—give us help with these kinds of questions? Yet, these are the questions that reflect the existential condition of man with both his rationality and his irrationality.

Some of us see in this situation a crucial role for education. Clearly, it calls for a redefinition of schools as agencies for the reconstruction and humanization of society. With such a view of the role of the school, one could then begin to project a framework for tackling the specifics of the dilemma posed by this teacher.

Problem 8 (continued)

8–12.   (Individual)

Current trends in society seem to be de-humanizing us all. In a sense we are all becoming disadvantaged. In what ways is this so?

8–13.   (Individual)

What social changes are needed to afford a maximum opportunity for the personal development of the American lower-middle, and middle classes? Would these changes be compatible with the needs of the poor?

8–14.   (Individual)

What is the potential role of education in resolving these problems?

8–15.   (Individual)

What is the obligation of the teacher in improving education?

8–16.   (Individual)

What obligation does the teacher carry toward the larger questions of social renewal?

8–17.   (Individual)

How do you, as a teacher, plan to face the complex series of personal and professional challenges raised here?

Crisis in the System

How deep, how widespread is the school crisis? Charles Silberman has provided one of the most exhaustive studies of this question. His work, *Crisis in the Classroom,*[15] has emerged as a major focal point of discussion. It has excited the interest of educator and citizen alike. As a future teacher you will find reading Silberman's carefully drawn document an important event in your education.

The following review[16] of *Crisis in the Classroom* is presented with a dual purpose. The review, by itself, provides evidence that there is a system-wide crisis of increasing social concern—a crisis which has a bearing on your own aspirations. In addition, the author hopes that this review will encourage you to read Silberman's work.

What are schools for? The traditional answer comes in two parts: Schools convey knowledge and skills to the young so that some day they can get good jobs; and schools introduce the young to their cultural heritage so that they can participate in the country's social and political life.

The trouble with the first part of this answer is that we're no longer sure *what* knowledge and *which* skills adequately prepare young people for the job market. Little correlation exits between training and performance, and the particular vocations for which the young are today prepared may no longer exist or may be radically altered by the time they're ready to practice them.

The trouble with the second part is that the broader purpose of the schools —to guarantee future carriers of the culture—is now widely discredited among the young themselves, who doubt the validity of our institutions and hence the necessity for perpetuating them. They don't want to fill predetermined slots in the society, and they resent the cloistered exercises that in fact keep them quarantined from society.

Besides, the radical young argue, schools devoted chiefly to job preparation and socialization are essentially anti-life, for their secondary effect (sometimes, it seems, their primary intent) is to inculcate docility, suppress curiosity and atrophy the senses. Surburban schools may be better than slum schools in transmitting the basic skills needed to find decent jobs. But they may be worse in discouraging individuality—simply because they control their students more completely.

Those who think I overstate should read *Crisis in the Classroom* by Charles Silberman, an editor of *Fortune* magazine and author of the much-praised *Crisis in Black and White.* Silberman is not a man who is anyone's idea of an "extremist." Yet his book is a formidable indictment of all levels of education in this country. And a masterly one: thorough and well-informed (somewhat less so about the universities than the primary and secondary schools), combining firsthand observation with a remarkable grasp of the vast

---

[15]Charles Silberman, *Crisis in the Classroom* (New York: Random House, Inc., 1970).

[16]Martin Duberman, "Crisis in the Classroom," *New York Times Book Review* (September 20, 1970), © 1970 by The New York Times Company. Reprinted by permission.

literature on education, characterized throughout by a methodical, almost legalistic respect for evidence and an even-handed, dispassionate tone.

The sum of his argument is that our schools are failing to meet *any* of the standards by which successful education is usually gauged: the accumulation of information and skills, independence of opinion, continuing curiosity, an appreciation for the affective side of life and the ability to translate insight into action.

In terms of all these standards, Silberman demonstrates (through an extended analysis of the English primary schools) the superior effectiveness of "informal" education, an inclusive term for a phenomenon known by many names, including "free" schools, "open" schools and the "integrated curriculum." Such education starts with "a conception of childhood as something to be cherished," and proceeds from the conviction "that learning is likely to be more effective if it grows out of what interests the learner, rather than what interests the teachers."

In 1967 a British Parliamentary Commission known as the Plowden Committee issued a now famous report on informal education, urging that it be adapted by all English primary schools. Silberman applauds most of that report—especially its insistence that the years spent in educational institutions must themselves be regarded as important (not merely as stepping stones to somewhere else) and that a learning community must guarantee that children will "live first and foremost as children and not as future adults."

Yet Silberman thinks the Plowden report "exaggerates" in its statement that "the best preparation for being a happy and useful man and woman is to live fully as a child." It's the same exaggeration, he feels, from which the progressive-school movement in this country suffered in the 1920's and 1930's, and from which certain writers on education (A. S. Neill, John Holt, Carl Rogers, Paul Goodman, George Dennison, Edgar Friedenberg) suffer today. Silberman refers to these writers glancingly at a number of points, calling them "romantics"—a term which successfully conveys opprobrium, but not the reasons for it. Silberman is eager to separate himself from the "romantics," yet fails to clarify the grounds on which he does so. This is an intriguing phenomenon to me, since I'm in deep sympathy with Neill and Holt, and have long been puzzled by the reactions of men like Silberman— humane, optimistic, acute—who somehow cannot cross (can hardly name) the mysterious divide.

Silberman often sounds much like Neill and Holt—and the radical young whose sentiments bisect theirs at so many points. He laments the joylessness of most schools. He insists on the necessity of play. He is furious that schools are preoccupied with order and control, with inculcating chronic dependence while claiming they are busy about the Lord's work of making individuals. He knows that our schools have long been *political* institutions (rather than having been recently politicized by radicals), which is to say he knows that the schools control the gateways to affluence and power in this society. And he knows that, far from being equalizing institutions, they perpetuate the society's inequities by sorting out "unacceptable" children—sorting them so rigidly that their access to opportunity is permanently blocked.

In all of this, Silberman's description of our schools is much of a piece with the diagnosis offered by men like Neill or Holt. It is in prescribing for the school's ills that Silberman's psychological distance from those men becomes apparent. He simply doesn't trust children (which is to say, human nature) to the same extent that they do. Nor is he as comfortable as they are with the proposition that personal contentment is *the* goal of life, *even* if that must come at the expense of "productivity."

Silberman argues—placing himself squarely in the tradition of Comenius and against that of Rousseau—that "nature" provides the basis for education, but does not make formal education unnecessary. He rejects the contention that the child will develop to best advantage if allowed simply to follow his own instincts and interests. But he argues on too abstract a level, never really spelling out when he thinks a child should be let alone and when guided. Neill and Holt don't think it's wise, either, to let children do *anything.* Instead of suggesting that they do, Silberman might better have focused on the particular areas in which he feels they are excessively permissive. Had he been that concrete, he would have clarified the differences between himself and the "romantics" and driven the *basic* argument forward.

By leaving his differences with Neill and Holt vague, Silberman implies an impassable gulf. This is the more curious because ordinarily he deplores dichotomies of opinion and does all he can to avoid them. In fact, his most characteristic stance in the book is to deny the necessity of either-or propositions. He searches always for what he calls a "tenable middle ground" in the debate on education—with the attendant danger of trying to recast every issue in that debate in such a way as to persuade us that no issues are involved and hence no choices are necessary.

In place of choice, he canonizes something he calls "right balance." He argues that freedom and structure are "perfectly compatible"; that much of what is taught is not worth knowing, but much of what is worth knowing can be taught; that children must be allowed to make discoveries, but teachers must discourage "purely random activity"; that the young are right to feel helpless in the face of antiquated rules and bureaucratic manipulation, but "it is the burden of choice that really torments or frightens them." Silberman's heart is so much in the right place; if only he would let it beat.

It's always easier to declare for "right balance" than to specify the properties by which it can be recognized. It would be difficult, for example, to disagree with Silberman's statement that "all students need some knowledge of the past if they are to understand the present and aspire to the future," but no teacher of history would find that dictum of much use when trying to decide *what* history to teach in *which* ways. Silberman does show a rare capacity for staying with particularities; his book is full of close description of specific experiments. But when he swings off on his abstract, compulsive search for the Holy Grail of "right balance," particularities depart and a heavy piety settles on the prose.

Besides, balance is not always a virtue. Nor is seeing merit in all positions. Temperateness can conceal (especially from oneself) an absence of position and an unwillingness to explore the reasons for that absence. Positions are hard to come by these days, and often suspect when found. But it is Silberman who has reminded us that whenever anyone discusses the "aims of education," he is inescapably dealing in the basic question, "What kind of human beings and what kind of society do we want to produce?" Dealing, in other words, in images of man.

No writer on education has a fully developed image of how human beings must, can or should behave, and the partial images they do have are always subject to challenge. But men like Neill and Holt have made more of an effort than Silberman to outline the premises and examine the ramifications of the particular model of human behavior implicit in their work. Most of Silberman's energies have gone instead to detailing the current horrors of the schools. And on that level, no book has done a better job.

Crisis in the Classroom is scrupulous and sensible, exhaustive in its scholarship, humane in its judgments. If not itself life-giving, it stands firmly against the life-destroyers. And that is a great deal, when surrounded by death.

Problem 9

9–1. (Individual)

What are the five most crucial problems identified by Silberman?

9–2. (Individual)

What are the causes of the problems you have identified?

9–3.   (Individual)

In the review of the Silberman report, can you detect solutions or directions to solutions to the five problems you identified?

9–4.   (Groups of Eight)

There are many dimensions to the problems identified in this study. Perhaps the one of greatest concern is the problem of teachers as subservient employees who tend to feel trapped in the system. Play the "Perplexity" game in order to become familiar with the pressures and feelings teachers face. As you play you will notice apparent irrationality of the system as it affects the teacher. This is the heart and purpose of the game. Consider it carefully in your end of the game class discussion. Also consider whether the schools in your particular area are as depicted here.

PERPLEXITY[17]

Overview

This game is played with six to eight players. Its purpose is to allow the participant an opportunity to make decisions similar to those in a normal school day. Any benefits from playing this game should come from the discussion and interaction of the total group.

This game allows for real situations to be injected into the group while still allowing involved persons to remain anonymous.

Materials

One die, situation cards (see pages 90–96), principal role sheet (see page 89). Situation cards should be shuffled and placed face down on the table. Players draw one for each teacher situation role they play. (Note: You may reproduce your own cards on heavier stock.)

Rules

Two members of the group act in two different roles: 1. the teacher; 2. the principal. To begin, one group member can elect or by agreement go first. This member plays the teacher role and rolls the die.

If the die lands on an *even* number, the player (teacher role) is awarded +1 point and may roll again or pass. One point is awarded until an uneven number is thrown. When this occurs, the player (teacher) must take a situation card.

The player to the immediate left becomes the principal and rolls die to determine which "principal" role he *must* play in regard to "teacher's" recommendation regarding his or her "situation."

---

[17]Mark Brown, Josephine L. Hall, James A. Stoffler, Kitti Culver, Donald G. Johnston, and M. W. Nickel. Unpublished game developed by a team of professors and administrators in a work shop conducted by the author and Dr. Warren I. Paul, St. Louis, 1971.

Example

The teacher rolls an uneven number, thus must take top situation card—player on left rolls die and it stops at 3. This player must play the role of Principal "Fearful Fred." *This is unknown to the group; this 3 die rolled by the Principal must not be seen by others.*

Thus the principal and the teacher have been decided and the situation drawn is read aloud to total group. The teacher has two minutes to respond as she normally would to the situation.

The principal then awards points according to match. Example: If teacher recommends strict punishment and the principal is #1 (extreme liberal Theodore), principal awards teacher −5 points.

One exception to principal's awarding points is #6 (Willie) who cannot decide how to award points.

Scale For Points

$$+5, +4, +3, +2, +1, 0, -1, -2, -3, -4, -5$$

Perfect agreement   Total disagreement

Note

1. It is the teacher's responsibility to convey or communicate sufficiently to the principal the handling of the situation in order that he may award points. In answering the situation, the teacher says, "This is the action I will take or recommend."
2. Also, the principal *must* not conceal the role he played in awarding of points.

After points have been awarded, the group tries to guess role of principal and may challenge any decision by teacher or principal at this time; however, points cannot be changed. (Play moves in counter-clockwise order.)

Score

One player is selected to keep score and inform players aloud of his progress.

−10 Player not approved for salary raise
−20 Player not recommended for tenure
−30 Player put on probation as teacher
−40 Player loses job
+40 Player becomes head of department or grade level and receives 6% pay increase
+30 Player receives merit pay increase plus 6% raise in salary
+20 Player receives approval for continuing contract plus 6% raise in salary
+10 Player receives 6% raise in salary

Situations

Players may use the situations included here or they may be composed by any group: ex-students, teachers, or principals.

Principals' Roles (Determined by roll of die)

1. "Do Your Own Thing Theodore": Extreme liberal. Always supports openness and freedom of learner (child).
2. "Permissive Pete": Moderate liberal. Takes into consideration all possibilities and tends to support an innovative staff.
3. "Fearful Fred": Moderate conservative. Takes solution that makes everyone happy—makes less waves.
4. "Authorative Arthur": Extreme conservative. Advocates law and order, maintains tradition through teacher dominance.
5. "See Saw Sam": Makes any decision. No explanation or rationale given for decisions made.
6. "Wishy Washy Willie": Makes no decision. Never says anything commital—awards no points.

The use of humorous names given to principals in this game is in no way intended to reflect on the role of the principal in the schools. This role is of ultimate importance for leadership in our school organization. Each of us knows these are types of personalities which could be and are found in any organization and within our society.

1. There is frequently enough noise from the classroom next to yours to disturb the activity of your class.

2. Clarence is a student who generally functions in the bottom quarter of your general math class. His intelligence is about average and he can be considered a normal boy in his social behavior. Clarence has a habit of not doing his homework.

3. Parent requests permission for early dismissal for personal reasons.

4. You are requested to take part in presenting a new sex education course to the students in your school. Sex education has never been offered in your school before and you have had very little training or experience for teaching it.

5. You ask Frank, a boy who has frequently given you trouble in the past, to take his seat at the beginning of the period so that work can begin. Frank says, "Kiss my ass!"

6. Joe is on probation. He has been visiting his probation officer regularly, but his father has just gotten a job and Joe no longer has transportation to get to the probation office. The probation officer asks you if he can visit Joe in school on a regular basis. If you agree, Joe will miss your class.

7. Students request to take field trip related to lesson.

8. Several students reported at home the references and comments you made as well as the "funny" story you told in class yesterday. Parents have objected strongly and threaten to speak to your principal.

9. Brad, a very ambitious boy who needs much teacher attention and recognition, torments the girl in the next desk. He is willing to do negative things, if necessary, to attract the attention he must have to satisfy his ego.

10. Rose is a bright girl who is bored in class, as her teacher refuses to give her work geared to her ability. She comes to you in a similar class and asks for help, which you give outside of class time. Now she refuses to return to her regular class.

11. You have reserved the school television set for your class to view a school telecast. The television set is shared by eight classrooms. At the appointed time, you find that another teacher has taken the television set to her classroom.

12. José responds to a question during class discussion in social studies with an answer in Spanish. He is an average student academically, but generally quiet and withdrawn in class.

13. Johnny, a mischievious child, requests permission to go to the restroom during class.

14. Teacher punishes female adolescent student by sending student to principal's office for a major offense. Parents object, request that child be spanked like the boys.

15. Two or three of your better students in a required social studies class stay after school to request that they be allowed to substitute an individual research project for approximately six weeks of normal classroom activities.

16. Parents object to strict criteria used by teacher in the grading process.

17. Several parents complain about student teachers' "hippie" appearance.

18. School board elections are to be held within the next few weeks. A member of the community takes out a petition to run for election to fill a vacancy. You have valid information that should prohibit his election.

19. Mary Jane refuses to take part in lab.

20. John flatly tells teacher to shut up and go to hell.

21. Betty refuses to bring necessary supplies to class—you know she can afford them.

22. Teachers require gym shorts for physical education classes—parent objects.

23. Teacher's class procedure is disrupted by female student not wearing undergarments and shoes.

24. Teacher is sponsor for club. Club elects to sponsor a dance—a religious group objects to teacher.

25. Club sponsor lets students sell candy to earn money—student refuses to return money or candy to club after quitting. Other students object to teachers.

26. English teacher uses *The Scarlet Letter* for example of short story—parents object.

9–5. (Role Play Game: Entire Class)

Many schools use democratically organized faculty meetings to get at school problems. This method has limitations. Play "Black Angels" in order to get an idea of the weaknesses of the current faculty decision-making procedures. This activity will take most of the period.

BLACK ANGELS' PROTEST
Professors Role As School Board Member
Directions for Game

Your Name:	Calvin Smith
Situation:	As outlined in the principal's Bulletin to Teachers (pp. 99–100)
Directions:	1. Assign the following special roles to students. Try to match their current activities to the role they will play. The remainder of the class acts as faculty.

      a. Principal
      b. Vice Principal
      c. Counselor
      d. Student Protest Leader
      e. Conservative Mathematics Teacher

2. Hand out "special role" information to appropriate students.
3. Hand out Bulletin to Teachers to all class members (reproduce in quantities needed).
4. Position all players:
      a. Principal in front of room faces faculty.
      b. Vice-principal to left rear of principal.
      c. Counselor in middle of faculty.
      d. Student protest leader to side or rear, preferably out of sight but able to hear meeting.
      e. Mathematics teacher with other mathematics teachers.
      f. Other "faculty" to be loosely grouped by discipline. Some players may have to be "assigned" a discipline to achieve faculty "balance."
6. Your role is that of an observer. You represent ultimate power but cannot exercise power alone.
7. *Pass telephone messages to principal at proper time during the meeting* (see pp. 105–7 for messages).
8. Whether and when the student protest leader is brought into the meeting, and how long he stays, is up to the principal.

Conduct of Meeting:	As done by the principal. Start will be 3:00 P.M. by "game time."

*End of
  Meeting:*

At 3:40 P.M. game time, 40 minutes after the meeting begins, unless a decision is reached sooner.

*Professor's
  Evaluation:*

If applicable, mention the following during game evaluation:
1. Any decision made will not be backed by everyone.
2. So the real issue, if a split occurs, is:
   a. Go for a power play.
   b. Do what's perceived as right.
3. In many districts, initiation for administrative action comes from higher administrative levels.
4. This situation is a classic example of: If the power structure is supported, rapport with students will be destroyed.
5. Probable result: Nothing was done, and the students marched anyway. They returned to school the following day.
6. Opportunity for questions.

Overview:

The *true* problem (and it's not obvious) is what happened even weeks before the incident. All one can do now is to convince people (e.g., students) that past decisions were wrong, and that you, as the administration or "establishment," will change and go a new way. Granted, this is only a reaction to a symptom, but it may buy time for a more lasting solution.

WESTSIDE HIGH SCHOOL

Tuesday

BULLETIN

TO: All Teachers

FROM: Thomas Strate, Principal

SUBJECT: Today's Disturbance

As you know, classes were suspended at 12:37 today and school was dismissed following the student disturbance in the cafeteria at which Mr. Jenkins was severely injured. (He was taken to General Hospital.)

Now the students are demanding to be allowed complete control over the assembly scheduled for tomorrow. I have not acceded to their demand, of course, but I feel you should be involved in whatever decision is finally made. Accordingly, I have called this 3:00 P.M. emergency faculty meeting which you are now attending.

Particularly for our newer teachers, here is background information you should know:

1. Mr. Smith is representing our school board. He has asked me to announce that he will not interfere with our professional decisions. We are, of course, subject to all of the responsible administrative agencies, such as the superintendent, board of education, state department of education, etc. Any suspension of classes must be temporary only, for unless the school is operated continuously during the school year our state funds will be cut off. We have 2,000 students enrolled in this high school.

2. Traditionally, and in line with the best American educational ideals and this state's multiracial and multiethnic population composition, our assemblies have presented both or all sides, if more than one, of whatever topic is on the program. Student suggestions for topics and/or to present assemblies usually have been honored, especially if they have been submitted in triplicate and according to the established procedures.

3. Yesterday a group of students submitted properly a request to present an anti-racism assembly program this week or next. I called in the students who signed the request and asked them what they intended to cover in the program. It developed that they wished to include only anti-establishment criticisms. I pointed out that Westside High School has had a tradition of presenting balanced views, so that the program should include positive viewpoints. The students replied that while most assemblies did have balanced programs, which they appreciated, all the patriotic assemblies they'd ever had were purely racist

and criticisms by blacks were never allowed. Of course, I said, that was in keeping with the school board's policies as to support of our nation. Further, there are public relations considerations, I told them; what would parents and others say if they thought we were teaching anti-Americanism? They rejected that, saying that it was time somebody "told it like it is" to the students, and that the school board and the parents had better learn the "facts," too. Since they refused to present a balanced position, naturally I refused their assembly request.

As a result, during lunch period today, a large number of students created a major disturbance in the cafeteria, damaging school property and injuring Mr. Jenkins. The students, who seem to be led by Fred Jones, a senior in the college preparatory sequence, now demand to present their program at tomorrow's assembly or else they will march on the school.

Your ideas will be appreciated.

Thomas Strate
Principal

Principal's Role

Your Name: Thomas Strate

Situation: As outlined in your Bulletin to Teachers. You are worried. It is 3:00 P.M. Tuesday. You have just been informed that a representative of the School Board, and possibly other officials, will be present at the meeting to observe.

You and the board members are afraid that if the students do not receive permission for their assembly, they will not only march, they will also riot in the streets and maybe try to burn or damage the high school. You have just learned that the Mayor will go on television and radio at 4:00 today—in less than one hour—to discuss the situation and to announce whether he will or will not call out the National Guard to maintain order tomorrow morning. Thus, the school board member will be pressing you for a decision by 3:40 so that he will have time to telephone it to the Mayor.

Other Factors:
1. Newsmen have been barred from the meeting.
2. However, to help clarify the situation, you have asked Fred Jones, the student protest leader, to wait in the next room in case you feel he should be invited in to interact with the teachers; he is there now, and you suddenly realize he probably can hear the meeting through an air duct between the two rooms.
3. Mr. Jenkins, the injured teacher, as of 2:30 P.M. was in "satisfactory" condition in General Hospital.

Support: Being fairly newly appointed as principal, you do not yet know your faculty well enough to identify differing viewpoints. Your vice-principal is beside you, however, and you know he is a hard-liner. Also, you know your counselor is popular with the students and has helped many of them effectively.

Your Mission: Conduct the meeting.

Objectives:
1. Decide a course of action.
2. Obtain a faculty support.
3. Restore harmony and communications with students.
4. Keep community calm—retain community support.

Vice-Principal's Role

Your Name: Cyrus Jones

Situation: As outlined in the principal's Bulletin to Teachers and what he has told you.

Your Personality:	You are responsible for school discipline and order. You are a hard-liner from the old school, happiest when students do as they are told, quietly. You feel students are being allowed to have too much freedom. Thus, you are essentially authoritarian, although in disciplinary situations you always strive to ascertain exactly what happened so as to be fair. In any student-teacher situation, however, you invariably support the teacher.
Your Responsibility:	Support the principal in a way that will maintain discipline and order. "We must maintain our position of authority."
Note:	Two windows in your car were broken and two tires were slashed during the disruption. You are mad about that. You personally fought with three students, two black and one white. All three left school promptly.

Counselor's Role

Your Name:	Ellen Fine
Situation:	As outlined in the principal's Bulletin to Teachers.
Your Position:	You like the students, and most of them like you and often come to you with their problems. You are very distressed by this whole affair, because you feel, in all fairness and good citizenship, that the students have a point. Yet you can see the school's view, too, and you are a good friend of Ron Jenkins, the injured teacher.
Your Objective:	Provide an avenue to restore, maintain, and increase communications and trust between the students and the administration and faculty, even if this seems to you to mean advocating a lenient attitude toward the students.

You were in the cafeteria and saw Mr. Jenkins hit by a food tray and pushed through a glass door. You estimate that about 250 students, boys and girls, were involved. Among other things, you saw Sue Smith, a white girl, pour her milk over Miss Williams' hair. Miss Williams is a black teacher. |

Math Teacher's Role

Your Name:	Bill Hawkins
Situation:	As outlined in the principal's Bulletin to Teachers.
Your Position:	You are a tenured mathematics teacher, highly structured in viewpoint. A veteran of the Korean War, in which you won a Bronze Star medal for heroism in combat, you are highly patri-

otic. You are assistant commander of the local VFW (Veterans of Foreign Wars) post, and you resent criticism of the United States and what you feel it stands for. Ron Jenkins, the injured teacher, is a good friend of yours.

Your Apprehension:

Late this afternoon you heard that the students planned to display amnesty and Communist anti-U.S. posters at the assembly they requested. You also heard that they were going to bring in weird speakers and a couple of folk singers to sing anti-American songs, and that next time they were going to try to have assemblies for the cop-killing Black Panthers, and maybe even some kind of pornographic sex education, or abortion, or something. This kind of thing can corrupt our kids fast, you believe. Incidentally, you're a firm believer that spanking with a paddle or strap is good even for older adolescents. (After all, *you* were raised that way, and it hasn't hurt *you* any.)

You have heard, from reliable sources, that several conservative groups *will march tomorrow* to the school, unless the students are punished. You fear even further problems if the assembly is granted. Someone tore up your grade book while you were at lunch. While at lunch, you saw two black students beating a white girl, Sue Smith. You are highly emotional but unorganized and defensive of your views.

Student Protest Leader's Role

Your Name:

Fred Jones (you prefer "Monk")

Situation:

As outlined in the principal's Bulletin to Teachers, a copy of which you have managed to obtain. You have agreed to wait in the room next to the meeting in case the principal feels you can clarify certain points for the teachers. It develops that you can hear the entire meeting through an air duct between the two rooms.

Other Factors:

You are a senior in the college preparatory sequence, with an A average. Until now, you have been fairly content with the high school and its curriculum and teachers, although not always happy with areas of curriculum you and other students feel lack "relevance" and with the school's rules and disciplinary measures, some of which you see as too strict. In all of this, you are supported by the large majority of students, although most haven't been really uptight about anything until this assembly issue.

Now you—and they—have almost spontaneously become very militant, and all of you fully intend to march tomorrow if your demands are not met. Admittedly, with regard to student militancy, you have not thought much past this assembly issue. *You are convinced that black people are not making progress, and, as a black, you are impatient.*

You feel that the school has lost credibility and that students' faith in the school cannot be reestablished without a major concession such as the assembly. You point out that the administration has already overstated its position and is racist. You were at the lunchroom crisis and saw Mr. Jenkins hit three students about ten minutes before the counselor entered the room. You will report back to students.

IMPORTANT MESSAGE

FOR *Mr Strate*

DATE _____ TIME *3:16* A.M. P.M.

WHILE YOU WERE AWAY

M *Sgt. Price*

OF *City Police*

PHONE No. _____ AREA CODE _____ NUMBER _____ EXTENSION

TELEPHONED		PLEASE CALL	
CALLED TO SEE YOU		WILL CALL AGAIN	
WANTS TO SEE YOU		RUSH	
RETURNED YOUR CALL			

MESSAGE *For your information A group of Black students have set fire to a garbage can 9 blocks from here. No danger to school.*

SIGNED *RY*

LITHO IN U.S.A.

IMPORTANT MESSAGE

FOR *Mr. Strate*

DATE _____ TIME *3:25* A.M. P.M.

WHILE YOU WERE AWAY

M *Sgt. Price*

OF *City Police*

PHONE No. _____ AREA CODE _____ NUMBER _____ EXTENSION

TELEPHONED		PLEASE CALL	
CALLED TO SEE YOU		WILL CALL AGAIN	
WANTS TO SEE YOU		RUSH	
RETURNED YOUR CALL			

MESSAGE *A group of white students have congregated in a drug store two blocks from here. There appears to be no danger.*

SIGNED *AB*

LITHO IN U.S.A.

IMPORTANT MESSAGE

FOR *Mr. Strate*

DATE _____ TIME *3.30* A.M. P.M.

WHILE YOU WERE AWAY

M *Jennifer Wilson*

OF _____

PHONE No. _____ AREA CODE _____ NUMBER _____ EXTENSION

TELEPHONED		PLEASE CALL	
CALLED TO SEE YOU		WILL CALL AGAIN	
WANTS TO SEE YOU		RUSH	
RETURNED YOUR CALL			

MESSAGE *About 150 black students have set up a camp on the football field for the night. They have a bonfire.*

SIGNED *AB*

LITHO IN U.S.A.

IMPORTANT MESSAGE

FOR *Mr. Strate*   TIME *3:30*   A.M. P.M.

DATE_____

WHILE YOU WERE AWAY

M *Coach Perkins*

OF_____

PHONE No._____ AREA CODE _____ NUMBER _____ EXTENSION

TELEPHONED		PLEASE CALL	
CALLED TO SEE YOU		WILL CALL AGAIN	
WANTS TO SEE YOU		RUSH	
RETURNED YOUR CALL			

MESSAGE *The Puerto Rican students have broken into and are occupying the temporary classrooms behind the football field.*

SIGNED *AB*

LITHO IN U.S.A.

IMPORTANT MESSAGE

FOR *Mr. Strate*

DATE_____   TIME *3:30*   A.M. P.M.

WHILE YOU WERE AWAY

M *Security Officer Moore*

OF_____

PHONE No._____ AREA CODE _____ NUMBER _____ EXTENSION

TELEPHONED			
CALLED TO SEE YOU		PLEASE CALL	
WANTS TO SEE YOU		WILL CALL AGAIN	
RETURNED YOUR CALL		RUSH	

MESSAGE *The campus security agents are standing between the two protesting student groups.*

SIGNED *AB*

LITHO IN U.S.A.

IMPORTANT MESSAGE

FOR *Mr. Strate*

DATE_____   TIME *3:35*   A.M. P.M.

WHILE YOU WERE AWAY

M *Officer Moore*

OF_____

PHONE No._____ AREA CODE _____ NUMBER _____ EXTENSION

TELEPHONED		PLEASE CALL	
CALLED TO SEE YOU		WILL CALL AGAIN	
WANTS TO SEE YOU		RUSH	
RETURNED YOUR CALL			

MESSAGE *The campus security people have withdrawn and have called the police. The white students are marching on the school.*

SIGNED *AB*

LITHO IN U.S.A.

IMPORTANT MESSAGE

FOR _Mr. Strate_   TIME _3:38_ A. M. / P. M.

DATE_____

WHILE YOU WERE AWAY

M _Nielsen_

OF_____

PHONE No._____ AREA CODE _____ NUMBER _____ EXTENSION

TELEPHONED		PLEASE CALL	
CALLED TO SEE YOU		WILL CALL AGAIN	
WANTS TO SEE YOU		RUSH	
RETURNED YOUR CALL			

MESSAGE _Superintendent Nielsen has given police full authority and has ordered this building evacuated._

SIGNED _RB_

LITHO IN U. S. A.

IMPORTANT MESSAGE

FOR_____

DATE_____   TIME_____ A. M. / P. M.

WHILE YOU WERE AWAY

M_____

OF_____

PHONE No._____ AREA CODE _____ NUMBER _____ EXTENSION

TELEPHONED			
CALLED TO SEE YOU		PLEASE CALL	
WANTS TO SEE YOU		WILL CALL AGAIN	
RETURNED YOUR CALL		RUSH	

MESSAGE_____

SIGNED_____

LITHO IN U. S. A.

IMPORTANT MESSAGE

FOR_____

DATE_____   TIME_____ A. M. / P. M.

WHILE YOU WERE AWAY

M_____

OF_____

PHONE No._____ AREA CODE _____ NUMBER _____ EXTENSION

TELEPHONED		PLEASE CALL	
CALLED TO SEE YOU		WILL CALL AGAIN	
WANTS TO SEE YOU		RUSH	
RETURNED YOUR CALL			

MESSAGE_____

SIGNED_____

LITHO IN U. S. A.

9–6.   (Individual)

The essential reality in any human enterprise is that every participant has his own philosophic outlook. "Black Angels" reveals some basic differences in point of view that may occur in typical faculties. Describe four or five philosophic views that faculty members may hold regarding school operation as revealed by this activity.

9–7.   (Individual)

As long as faculty members hold diverse views and commitments about school operation, there is the danger that the various teachers will work at odds with each other in resolving problems. With respect to "Black Angels," describe the kind of independent action that faculty members are likely to take with regard to the problem at hand. Begin by identifying the philosophic basis in your answer which would lead to the action you describe.

9–8.   (Individual)

Can you find a common ground between these faculty perceptions and actions? Describe it.

9–9.   (Individual)

What would you do for the next two weeks if you were principal of the school in question?

9–10.   (Discussion: Groups of Five)

Compare your individual answers to this problem. Try to reach a concensus of proper action by the principal.

9–11.   (Task Groups of Four)

How could you contribute to the improvement of the system? List ways teachers can improve their own lot.

9–12.   (Total Class Discussion)

Share your answers to 9–11 and try to identify a way for faculties to move forward.

Why Is So Little Progress Being Made?

One of the worst implications of the Silberman report is that little progress is being made in solving education's problems. Why is it that, with so many teachers in this country, one sees so little change in schools? Why are the professors of education so ineffective in stimulating change? Why is it that the curriculum-building processes attempted in American schools have failed?

The obstacles in the path of school improvement are many. Yet, this author sees one difficulty as being particularly unfortunate. The accepted wisdom is that an educational program or curriculum is a planned, coordinated pedagogical vehicle designed to assure certain learning outcomes on the part of the student(s). A curriculum arises out of a philosophic base such as the Bible-oriented *divine wisdom* view, the classics-oriented *eternal truths* view, the democratic *social needs* perspective, or the scientific method as *universal tool* bias. The goals of a curriculum are carefully considered and adopted after suitable pondering. Objectives, content, selection, instructional strategy, evaluation, and assessment techniques all flow out of the adopted goals with the aid of curriculum and instructional technology as predictably as February follows January.

The previous process involves many people with the curriculum expert as facilitator. Parents, employers, students, teachers, counselors, administrators, even professors are represented. Once a plan adopted, the administrator moves heaven and earth to implement it so the teacher may faithfully assure student outcomes according to the blueprint.

The accepted wisdom as outlined above is not working. One wonders if it has ever worked anywhere except in experimental programs. Writer after writer has condemned the schools, saying in effect that educators are not doing what they claim. Our schools have been under fire for a long time. Goodman, Kohl, and now Silberman are but a few of the many names that have become synonymous with the thesis that educators saying that students are learning certain facts are in fact teaching students to hate school and all that it represents. *What is wrong?*

Within individual classrooms teachers often try to develop a curriculum and students often try to learn. Both parties engage in the teaching-learning process. They share a common intent—at least at the outset. There is ample documentation that students tend to lose their desire to learn as they progress through the system. Holt's *How Children Fail*[18] and Silberman's Carnegie Report, *Crisis in the Classroom,*[19] support this point amply.

This writer believes that teachers also lose interest and motivation as a result of living in the system. The statistics on the retention rate in the teaching profession are widely known and the Silberman report confirms that teachers are victims of the system. The lack of spirit shown by teachers in *Up the Down Staircase*[20] has been visible among many older teachers this writer knows. This writer's father, an educator himself, is quite convinced that decisions and trends within the system always or nearly always operate

---

[18]John Holt, *How Children Fail* (New York: Pitman Publishing Corporation), 1964.

[19]Charles E. Silberman, *Crisis in the Classroom* (New York: Random House, Inc.), 1970.

[20]Belle Kaufman, *Up the Down Staircase* (Englewood Cliffs, N.J.: Prentice-Hall Inc.), 1964.

to hamper learning. Many older teachers seem to be "keeping school" which, when pursued, turns out to be a way of saying "baby sitting." *What is wrong?*

A key to the answer to the problems of education may be to examine the source of decisions and policy changes in American schools.

Fact 1: *All power in the school structure rests in political institutions, i.e.:* school boards, legislatures, Congress, and the court system. Decisions and policy emanating from these bodies are the result of a political, not a pedagogical process.

Fact 2: *The power in the hands of American teachers is largely political, social, and economic.* The AFT and NEA, as expressions of unified teacher needs, act in all three areas, but the individual teacher is usually unable to find an expression for *his needs in his classroom.*

Fact 3: *The power of the public is political, economic, and social in nature.* The public elects representatives, mounts pressure group efforts, and passes on monetary issues. Too often decisions of the public are *votes against* rather than votes for something.

Fact 4: *Students have no power but are in the process of assembling a social power similar to that found in higher education.* Students may adopt civil and uncivil protest. Individual students, like individual teachers, may be unable to relate this trend to personal needs.

Fact 5: *Administrators are merely responding to the forces and problems they meet; they are not leading, nor are they influencing any of the political, economic, social elements described under Facts 1 through 4 above.*

This last point is the surface symptom that most concerns teachers. The superintendent gets it from the top. He is so busy and overworked that he cannot lead. He merely responds to crisis after crisis. In some places superintendents are not even putting out fires anymore. They are just running from fire to fire looking for ways to tackle one, some, or any of the problems. Carroll Hanson gives an excellent documentation of this point.[21]

The school principal receives orders from the central office, but these orders often take a back seat to the crises of the day. If the individual principal can act on the central office dictates, he probably just blindly implements them. Gone are the days when a principle could ponder orders and, if he felt them to be incorrect, propose a revision to the higher administration. The principal, like the superintendent, is fighting for life —his own and his school's. He is so busy dealing with problem people—students, teachers, parents, police, and trespassers—that he has little time left for the staff. Most of that remaining time is spent on logistic survival. The boiler has a problem and the central office has not sent a repair crew. The classrooms on the south wing of the third floor are too crowded and the schedules need to be reexamined. The new teachers can't

---

[21]Carroll Hanson, "In the Eye of the City," *Phi Delta Kappan* 52 (October 1970).

fill out the attendance report forms, and the older teachers refuse to do it at all. Unreal? Not at all. Cunningham documents this point very well on pages 17–27. His experiences as an exchange principal were very survival oriented.

Suppose that teacher A wants to obtain a decision from the principal so that he can better meet the needs of his students. Teacher B arrives with another request relative to his students. The requests conflict. What does the principal do? In more leisurely times he would weigh the merit of the arguments and decide on the best compromise in view of resources. This solution would be based upon the intent to provide the greatest pedagogical advantage to the largest number of students. Now that's not bad. Teachers and students can understand and accept resource limitations and the need to avoid conflict within the system. Results are not ideal, but they are acceptable.

But that's not how it works today. To be sure, principals, superintendents, and other administrators still try to resolve the conflict between resources, pedagogical demands, and outside pressures and problems. The tragedy is that we are in a period of change, perhaps revolutionary change, and the schools are in the middle. The decision-making processes are overloaded with conflicting demands and needs. One group demands bussing, another opposes it, and the court orders it as the clerk-treasurer announces he cannot find the funds to bus. Venereal disease and drug problems are on the rise to the point that resources need to be diverted to security measures within the schools. At the same time, some groups are demanding sex education. Other groups are demanding prayer, no sex, and rigid moral instruction. The teachers are going to strike if they don't get a pay raise, and the poll of voters portends a tax levy defeat. The state passes a law requiring schools to provide behind-the-wheel driver training and does not provide funds. Groups are on the march in and out of schools for this, against that. *How much concern can be given curricular problems?*

Even the teachers find they spend their energies controlling hall violence, identifying drug addicts, and taking cases of discipline, emotion, truancy, trespassing, and just plain illness to the office. Teachers are prone to say that "if I didn't have to worry about that institutional garbage, I would have time to teach."

American school administrators have by and large made a choice. In the face of limited resources and personal energy, in the face of rising pressure and problems, in the face of an impending system break, one must stick to basics:

Basic One: *No one will learn anything if the school as an institution is destroyed.* Therefore, go to any lengths to preserve the establishment.

Basic Two: *Teachers cannot teach if the classroom is a battleground.* Therefore, try with any remaining energy to reduce logistical, political, and social pressure on your teachers.

Administrators are no longer worrying about pedagogy. Don't blame them. If you were an administrator, you would accept need to survive as being paramount, just as they do. *What does all this mean?*

In the lower grades, the student usually deals with one teacher and is relatively well motivated. The teacher and student work out a curriculum for the year they are together. In the high school, the student has lost much of his motivation and deals with several teachers each day. The teacher and students attempt to work out a program for the fragment in which they are involved, but there is no one around to coordinate horizontally the curricular fragments. Further, there is no significant articulation of program from grade to grade. *Hence, the student progresses through an increasingly fractured curriculum as he moves from K through 12.* But this reality does not match the accepted wisdom: one cannot call fragmented experiences under 35 different teachers a program or a curriculum. Teachers know that the stuff taught in school is fragmented and repetitious, but they cannot change things without help from the administration and the *administration has no help to give.*

With the teachers surviving in their classrooms as best they can and administrators warding off pressures as best they can, one begins to wonder where the educational decisions are made. Then, when one sees textbooks adopted or rejected on political bases, one begins to fear that the following rule may be true:

NO EDUCATIONAL DECISION MADE OUTSIDE OF THE CLASSROOM IS EVER MADE ON A PEDAGOGICAL BASIS

Critics are bound to assert that this axiom is the result of a defeatistic outlook and cannot lead to a positive contribution to education. This writer is not at all pessimistic about the future in spite of his convictions about educational decision making. In fact, the principle advanced here can help us understand why curriculum reform has been such a failure, why professors (like this writer) have no effect on school operations, and why public school curriculum people fail to create change.

The educational community is schizophrenic; part of the community operates on one frame of reference and part on another. The curriculum specialists and teachers operate on a pedagogical basis, while all others on a reality oriented political-social basis. No progress can be made as long as this gap exists. Hence, there are three alternatives for the future:

Option One: Teachers can get the rest of the educational system and the public to shift its basis of operation to pedagogy.

This option is patently impractical and unrealistic. In fact, one of the problems of professors and supervisors may be an adherence to this view that the "whole world is wrong but me."

Option Two: Teachers can develop ways of operating between these bases and of "bridging" the gap.

The second option sounds good in theory, but is beyond the skills of many educators at the moment. It is likely, desirable, and possible that certain individuals can make this transition, but if they do this, option three becomes a key part of their scheme.

Option Three: Teachers can abandon their position and move into the political-social process.

The third approach is the most practical. Curriculum planners could design programs from the political-social view. Our integrity is preserved by using pedagogy in the form of criteria for the assessment of these programs. The technique would not begin with goal determination. Rather, it would begin with an assessment of reality—social, political, and institutional. Designs would be made from the outside in to the individual rather than the other way around. Criteria would remain very similar to the old technique, with the impact on the child remaining central.

In trying option three, we would confront the most vital issues first. For example, instead of first worrying about the individual discipline or single child, we would begin by acting on larger social issues such as the tendency for the school as an institution to function as a leadership selection agency.

Notice that the issue given as an example goes far beyond curricular content as now treated. Whether a child makes it to a position of leadership as an adult involves institutional security, the child's ability to cope with a complex institution, the health and social services support of the institution, as well as the content of the course work. It doesn't matter what poem the child reads if he is mugged in the hall or if he is denied admission to certain programs for political or social reasons. We must begin with this kind of large perspective and institutional view; *teachers can contribute to this view.*

The implementation of this approach would require that institutional models be evaluated in terms of impact *on* learning outcomes *for* the individual student. As long as the pedagogical outcome criteria include the formal and informal curriculum, the results should be realistic and practical as well as functional in the real world.

Does the foregoing imply that techniques of instruction, content organization, and pedagogy are unimportant? Not at all. The point is that program and environmental decisions are not made on a pedagogical base. Hence, pedagogy in its pure form is limited.

Problem 10

10–1.   (Discussion Groups of Seven)

Assume that you are a teacher who wants to change a school policy concerning textbooks. What processes do you use? Educational, economic, social, or something else?

10–2.   (Discussion Groups of Seven)

Comment on the theme of this article that educational decisions are not made on an educational basis. Do the Cunningham article and the Silberman report support the position expressed here?

10–3.   (Discussion Groups of Seven)

Schools are at the heart of the American culture. They are vital to all groups and subgroups of society. It seems likely that schools will be at the center of all political and social forces. It seems likely that there will always be a school crisis. What is the role of a teacher who is going to spend his career in an institution in perpetual crisis? Doesn't this reflect concern for education?

The Dimensions of the Current Crisis

One of the most basic 20th century realities is that nothing is more certain than change itself. Society is undergoing radical change in all areas, and no aspect of society is more subject to the pressures and tensions of change than the schools.

There has always been a crisis in the schools. Issues such as "Who shall be educated?" "Should schools offer vocational programs?" "What is the best approach to teaching style?" and "What is the best content emphasis?" have been debated for more than a century. At times, temporary resolution of an issue permitted schools to move forward. Yet, the same old issues always seemed to come back in new contexts.

Even the value of school as a social institution has been an eternal issue in American education. The charge that formal education is irrelevant is not new. Anti-intellectualism has been and will continue to be a part of American life, and its influence will continue to cycle up and down as time passes. The same is true of other influences.

There is, however, a growing conviction that there are new elements in the current crisis in education, new elements which make the present time more hazardous than before. What are these new elements?

1. There is a new awareness that we have not yet implemented the "American Dream."
2. There is a new spiritual awakening in the need to become a whole person.
3. There is a new awareness of the value of and humanity of all men and a corresponding new awareness of the folly of war.
4. There is a new awareness of long-term concerns and goals and a de-emphasis on the immature concern for short-term objectives.
5. There is a new awareness of man's limits within the total environment and a new awareness of the limits of control possessed by individuals and by the species.
6. There are signs of a period of uncertainty as the previous factors are assimilated into the culture; we seem to be entering a period of searching for new solutions.

Is it possible that the crisis in education is little more than an extension of the crisis in society? Probably so. And it has always been so. For, in America, the schools are uniquely tied to the fabric of society. This is why the new elements in the school crisis, as seen by this writer, are so similar to the new elements in the social crisis.

What do all these new elements mean to the crisis in America's society and schools? Perhaps an illustration can be made by discussing the transition of an individual from one stage of life to another. We will use a new teacher as the example.

The beginning teacher, during his first weeks in a regular assignment, becomes aware of many bits of data for the first time. He discovers the needs of his pupils. He learns of the limits of his resources. He discovers his weaknesses in discipline. He finds that motivation is a tough problem. He becomes aware of the full dimensions of the challenge of teaching. It is a shock, a severe shock. He feels fear and frustration. He is uncertain about the future. A real problem is in his crisis in confidence. If he can renew his efforts he can and will overcome the crisis.   The danger and tragedy of beginners in teaching is that too many people give up and leave the profession. They lack the will to fight and to win.

Perhaps this is the nature of the current crisis in society and in the schools. America has reached a new stage of national evolution. New realizations about unfinished business have emerged. We are shocked by the nature of our problems and we have a crisis in confidence.

As this writer looks at the list of new elements in our problems he finds comfort in the fact that our concerns are appropriate. Our perceptions about the unfinished business are correct. We can tell what should be done much better than ever before. The only question is whether or not we have the will to solve these problems. And within the schools, do the educators have the will to persevere?

We are not a nation of quitters. Our national record is one of perseverance, and there is no reason to suspect that this perseverance has been lost.

There is reason to be *confident about the ultimate results of the current crisis;* the schools of 1985 or 1990 will be much more effective than current schools. The teachers will be doing a better job and will foster better results in their students. It is even possible to predict the kind of school operation that will be common in 1990, but the short term is another matter.

The Seventies is a decade of transition. It stands to reason that there will be a lot of waivering and many false starts before the new trends are established. Short-term predictions are impractical.

Student teachers, then, need to keep in mind what is *right* with the schools. They need to remember what strengths and accurate awareness of problems can give. They need to keep their faith in the future.

The organization of this volume is from concrete problems in teaching toward solutions. This is done in order to capitalize upon the curriculum theories that students learn best when they generalize from concrete data. It is also done in order to provide you, the student teacher, with a better means of solving your instructional problems.

Teachers need to know the nature of the problems before they can solve them. The problems, however, also cause uncertainty on the part of the teacher. It is hoped that, by making student teachers aware of problems before they encounter them, they will be able to work out solutions ahead of time. Even if solutions are not forthcoming, the shock of facing problems will be made less severe. Perhaps the requisite confidence will be easier to acquire and the new teacher can resolve his problems faster and less painfully.

Problem 11

11–1.   (Individual)

It is the position of the author that the *realization that a problem exists* has two aspects for individuals and/or groups. First, there is a realization that problems are real, solutions must be sought, and that there is a danger of failure. Second, there is a basis for seeking a solution. What, according to your perceptions, are the current problems in education? List them according to priority.

11–2.   (Individual)

For three of the problems on your list, describe the directions you think education will have to take in solving these problems.

11–3.   (Groups of Four)

Discuss the results of 11–2 in your group. Develop a single list of predictions. Present these to your class.

11–4.   (Individual)

Some problems in education are beyond the control of the teacher as an individual. Some are subject to resolution within the classroom. Divide your list of problems into categories as shown below.

Problems Beyond Scope of Teacher

Example: riots or bombings

Problems Subject to Resolution in a Classroom

Example: weakness in student vocabulary

11–5. (Individual)

This volume will develop the area of resolving problems within the classroom. First, however, let's look at the large-scale problems. A teacher lives within a system. This system controls the professional life of a teacher, but a teacher can influence it. Describe three ways a teacher can assist the system in improving itself. Select one example from the public arena, one from professional involvement, and one from internal system contributions.

11–6.   (Individual)

Based on your answers to the previous questions, do you think the same teaching methods can be used in the future as have been used in the past? What is your obligation for learning innovative teaching methods? Justify your position.

Confidence As Well As Competence

A teacher needs to know how to teach, but he also needs to know that he knows. His competencies are useless without confidence.

A student must master certain knowledge before he can proceed to the professional level. But it's not enough that he have the skill; he must also be able to believe in his own ability to progress.

Schools, in too many places, are marked by a lack of confidence on the part of students, teachers, and administrators. The student teacher may be underendowed with both confidence and competence. He needs all the support he can get as he moves into his new role. Yet, American schools are not equipped to assist beginning teachers. They are not set up to renew the tattered confidence of beginners; the beginner must renew his own confidence.

How does one go about this? Part of the solution is to pursue competence to the point of certainty. Another approach is to become familiar with the problem and to understand that this recognition is a requisite first step solution. A third approach is to alter one's thinking patterns.

Americans have been guilty of overemphasis of the negative in recent years. A pint of beer in a quart bottle can be seen two ways (as can schools). We have said the bottle is half-empty, but *it is not only half-empty, it is also half-full!* America's schools are good, although they must be even better.

Why, then, has the first part of this volume shown the negative side of education? There are two reasons.

1. Teachers tend to find the first year of their professional career a tremendous shock. Beginners are naive and surprised at the full dimensions of reality. This author believes that the beginner needs to be made aware of reality prior to trial by fire.
2. Recognition of reality in full, including the unfinished business and problems, is necessary before a person can begin to cope and solve problems.

The next section of this book will treat the instructional process and include examples of good teaching techniques that work well within the present imperfect system.

3

Avoiding
Traditional
Pitfalls

The Rut and One Way Out

Often the student teacher falls into a trap wherein he imitates the methods he has seen used by teachers and professors in the past. This method would be sound if experienced teachers actually used the best techniques. However, Olson has shown that this is not the case. In fact, teachers seem to use the least effective strategies and methods of instruction.

In reporting objective data from 20,000 classrooms, the most extensive survey of American education ever undertaken in one study, Martin N. Olson states that:

> ... style of educational activity was the single strongest overall predictor (of quality achievement). As can be seen in the table, particularly high scoring styles were small group work, individual work, discussion, laboratory work, pupil report, and demonstration. Lowest scoring styles were lecture, question/ answer, seat work, tests, and movies. Note the teachers' heavy reliance on the less effective styles (% column). School systems could significantly improve their performance scores by increasing the *frequency* or *skill* with which the teachers employ the highest scoring styles.[1]

Of the many techniques of instruction teachers know how to use, they actually seem to use the wrong ones, according to the Olson data. Notice that methods ranked lower in effectiveness tend to result in passive student involvement while the higher ranked methods result in more active student involvement.

---

[1]Martin N. Olson, "Research Notes: Ways to Achieve Quality in School Classrooms: Some Definitive Answers," *Phi Delta Kappan* 53 (September 1971): 63–65.
[2]Based on Martin N. Olson, loc. cit.

Style of Educational Activity
Related to Pupil Performance and Frequency of Use

Effectiveness		Style	Frequency of Use	
Rank	Score		Rank	%*
1	9.80	Small Group Work	10	4
2	8.76	Individual Work	2	14
3	8.42	Laboratory Work	8	5
4	7.63	Discussion	4	11
5	7.50	Pupil Report	12	2
6	6.68	Library Work	—	—
7	5.60	Demonstration	9	4
8	4.72	Rehearsal	13	1
9	4.38	Other	6	9
10	3.96	Television	—	—
11	3.69	Question/Answer	1	19
12	2.17	Seat Work	3	11
13	1.32	Movie	11	3
14	1.16	Test	7	7
15	1.09	Lecture	5	10

*Percent of observed time. Column does not total 100% since percentages have been rounded off.

Notice that individual work and discussion are alone among the most effective methods in regular use. These are easy methods to use. The other most effective methods are hard to set up and require much pre-planning.

Having determined that active student involvement is better than passive involvement, some points need to be made about the active methods.

1. The active methods studied actually work in public schools; there is nothing unrealistic about their use.
2. The active methods retain a high degree of teacher goal determination; they are not examples of permitting students to run wild.
3. The active methods involve more teacher planning than the passive methods. This point implies that the teacher must work harder.
4. Simulation and gaming techniques were not included in the Olson study but are active methods which are likely to yield good results; they are, in some cases, already packaged for the teacher.

During your first year of teaching, you will be provided with a syllabus and some hints about lesson planning. From this information *you* will have to build the courses you teach. You cannot build courses loaded with the best methods overnight; it will take years.

The dynamic teacher begins by building better and more student-centered methods and finally arrives at a level of mastery which makes successful teaching possible. This process takes years and is very difficult. It is a process that you will find difficult to implement.

One type of teacher may find the pressures too great to develop games, demonstrations, and other good methods and materials. This type gets trapped into dull routines. Part of the cause of this trap is the teacher's lack of professional support and resources to overcome his plight. You do not want to be this kind of teacher.

There is another possibility, a possibility this text seeks to encourage. A student teacher may begin to build materials during his methods courses and during student teaching *while he has more time* and *access to expert help.* Then, when he begins to teach, he has things for students to *do* so they will learn. This novice teacher faces less pressure, has more immediate success, and will be able to learn about his students while watching them work.

This approach requires that the traditional survey of methods of teaching be replaced by an examination of certain key methods and preparation of workable instructional packages. This text pursues this approach, asking you to develop competence in simulation and gaming methods and materials for your own use. *You* will have ammunition to use when the time comes to teach. And the more ammunition you have, the more time you will have to learn about your students, about your subject, and about the things you want to teach.

You will notice a major focus on simulation and gaming instructional techniques throughout the remainder of this volume. There are several key purposes to this focus.

Under traditional methods, the teacher must perform two activities at once. He must present the lesson and he must observe the class to see how well both he and the students are doing. It is very difficult to do both tasks at once. Some teachers never learn how to present a lesson *and* observe the students. You, as a new teacher, do not want to be an example of the poor tortured math teacher who works on the board while the class does its own thing behind his back.

Simulation and gaming methods are helpful at your career development stage. Nearly all of the planning is done before class and the lesson is merely a matter of giving a few directions to the students. You will have time to observe the students in your class without worrying about the lecture and myriad other items. You have opportunity, then, to observe your class during simulations and games, to determine more about them as people and more about their academic strengths and weaknesses. Take advantage of this time.

Another factor in the selection of simulation and gaming in the remainder of this text is the fact that simulation and gaming is a vital method you will not often observe in public school experiences. It is a sample of how different teaching can be.

In chapter 4 you will find a "Teaching Strategy Selector" which assists you in avoiding the same old traditional methods of teaching and their consequent pitfalls. These methods will serve as a concrete means of avoiding monotonous repetition of the same old techniques. And, if there is anything that causes more trouble to the beginning teacher than the inability to add variety and interest to his classes, it would be hard to identify.

The format of this section of this text will continue to be focused upon your involvement with your instructor and peers. Rather than activities aiming at awareness, the problems will be aimed at building skills and materials for instructional use.

Communication: The Heart of the Teaching-Learning Process

The Nature of the Process

The teaching-learning process is essentially one of communication. Moreover, the burden of the communication process falls upon you as a teacher, for your students are, by definition, less mature and less skilled in communicating than you. The recent development of micro teaching has been due in part to the realization that teacher education has not been treating the classroom communication process adequately and that active skill development is an important element in mastering the complexities of communicating with children. This section will discuss this aspect of teaching, but you should be aware of the element of communication skill development that is interwoven throughout the remainder of this text.

Many teachers, especially beginning instructors, are essentially lonely, anxious people. This is certainly not the result of isolation, for around them are many others with similar feelings: teachers and students who are also lonely and anxious. They have problems in communicating with others.

Jersild[3] argues that you cannot become an effective teacher until you can accept yourself. He states that the loneliest person is the person who is not at home with his own thoughts.

Have you noticed how many people fear having their voices recorded? If you have been part of an audio- or video-recorded micro teaching effort, you were probably nervous about being recorded. Such fear is, in part, because you have not yet seen or heard yourself as others see you. Such fear is normal, but it must be overcome if you are to accept yourself and become more open to others. The only way to do this is to look at yourself as others look at you on a regular basis. Regular use of audio and video taping equipment is vital.

The activities in this section appear to be and are skill development activities, but you need to understand that effective communication is deeper than that. The hope is that these activities will help you begin a process of self-awareness and self-acceptance which you will continue to develop throughout your education and career. Galloway points out:

> Assuming an open attitude toward self and others—the means for becoming better informed—involves awareness, understanding, and acceptance. To be aware is to observe more fully the nonverbal reactions of others and self. To understand implies the need to analyze the meaning of your observations and to suspend your judgements. To accept is to acknowledge that your behavior means what it does. This is especially difficult. Yet, once you accept what your behavior represents, the door is open to behaving differently. You

---

[3]Arthur Jersild, *When Teachers Face Themselves* (New York: Teachers College Press, 1954).

can come to terms with your own attitudes and feelings and you can begin to express yourself with real fidelity.[4]

Most novice teachers understand the need to make clear, interesting presentations. They work on skills which are first developed in the basic speech course most education students take, and they usually do a reasonable job of practicing these skills. But there is more.

Clarification

Teachers often find that the students did not understand what they said and there arises a need to clarify. Beginning teachers usually try to clarify by merely repeating themselves, and they get nowhere. You may have the same problem. Clarification is more than restating; it is also a process that requires changing words to synonyms students understand and, on occasion, selecting a completely new example. To get an idea of this process and to try your skills at clarification, play the following game.

Problem 12

Game: Groups of Five to Eight

CLARIFICATION GAME

The object of this game is to practice restating expressions to clarify them. Each round should last ten to fifteen minutes as determined by your instructor. Sit in a circle.

Rounds One and Two

1. Select a leader to start. He makes a statement similar to one a typical teacher would make. Example: "When supply drops and demand remains constant, prices tend to rise."
2. The person to the left of the leader assumes the role of clarifier and restates the same concept in *entirely different words.* The rest of the group makes a quick summary judgment about whether or not the second explanation was better than the first. Did it clarify the concept?
3. The same person (as in number 2 above) then makes up a new factual statement. Example: "Momentum increases according to the square of velocity."
4. The third person in the circle clarifies the statement of the second person, the clarification is judged, and a new statement is made. So on around the circle for two rounds.

---

[4]Charles M. Galloway, *Teaching is Communicating* (Washington, D.C.: Association for Student Teaching, Bulletin No. 29, 1970).

Rounds Three, Four, and Five

1. The leader makes a statement as in round one. This time he must clarify his own statement.
2. The second person makes a statement and then clarifies it. So on around the group.
3. Remember to judge each clarification statement as better or worse than the first one.

Asking Questions

It may be trite to state that communication is a two-way process, but the fact is that in too many classrooms the teacher does the talking. One reason is that teachers do not know how to draw the students into the process. The key is asking questions. If the first question fails to work, the teacher must be prepared to ask another question, one which clarifies the first and which makes the kind of response desired clearer. You will have to ask questions in your teaching. In fact, you may have to ask a whole series of questions before the students are certain how to respond. No amount of reading can give you this skill; hence, the following activity.

Problem 13

Game: Groups of Six to Eight

SOCRATIC TEACHING GAME

The Socratic Method is a unique method of teaching suitable for small group instruction in which the instructor encourages inductive student thinking and active student participation by means of questioning. The instructor restricts himself to asking sequential questions which lead to a conclusion. This game will give you a chance to try out this technique and, at the same time, encourage you to sharpen your questioning skills.

Planning for the Game

The day before you are to participate in the "Socratic Teaching Game," your professor will ask you to prepare a short five-minute lesson in an area of your own choice. As you prepare the lesson, you must restrict yourself to developing questions. *You will not be permitted to make any statements in the lesson.* If a person role playing the part of a student in your group asks you a question, *you must answer with a question.* In this situation you may choose to ask questions leading your questioner to his own answer or you may ask another participant to answer the question. Two special notes are important in planning for this game. First, be prepared to have a series of planned alternative questions. Second, limit your material; there is a danger of including too much material in this kind of lesson.

Directions

Your instructor will divide the class into groups of six to eight people. Designate a leader. He begins with a lesson. The rest of the group stops him when he slips and makes a statement. Since everyone is likely to make a statement in his first attempt at presenting a lesson, simply move to the next person on the left and have him give his lesson. After everyone in the group tries once, the leader may try his lesson a second time from the beginning. Your instructor may ask you to play this game two days in a row.

All statements are illegal, and when an "instructor" slips and makes a statement he is stopped and the next person tries his lesson. On subsequent attempts, the instructor must start over on his lesson. Continue until all lessons are complete. Use questions only.

Some Hints

In the "Socratic Teaching Game" you will have to develop content by asking questions. Therefore, the following types of questions will be helpful in planning. Try to prepare some questions that fit all the categories shown below.

1. *Extending:* asking students for more information or more meaning. For example, "What else could you say about that?"
2. *Justifying:* requiring the student to justify his response rationally. For example, "Would this be true in all cases?"
3. *Refocusing:* directing the students' or class' attention to a related issue. For example, "Is there any connection between that and —————? How would you compare that with —————?"
4. *Prompting:* cuing the student or giving hints. For example, "What else happened? What other chemicals would accomplish the same thing?"
5. *Redirecting:* bringing other students into the discussion by getting them to respond to another student's answer. For example, "How do you feel about John's answer? Can someone add to what John has said? Mary, do you feel John has covered that completely?"

Higher Order Questions

Communication with students involves more than merely getting them to talk. There is something wrong in the classroom where the teacher gets students to talk by the techniques developed earlier but in which the student talk is merely factual recall. Students need to do more than merely tell when "Columbus sailed the ocean blue." This aspect of communicating with students requires that they do higher order thinking, create new ideas, and then evaluate them.

You will find Norris Sanders' little book of great help in this area.[5] Not only does he explain questioning levels, but he also generates exemplar questions useful in your

---

[5]Norris M. Sanders, *Classroom Questions: What Kinds?* (New York: Harper & Row, 1966).

planning. You will need to raise both the level of your communication with students and the level of their thinking by increasing the sophistication of your questions. This is the purpose of the next activity.

Problem 14

Activity: Groups of Seven

QUESTION BUILDING

This written activity in which you practice raising the level of questioning is intended to sharpen your skill in avoiding the asking of rote questions.

Directions

After studying question levels below, assemble in groups of seven. To start the activity, each person is asked to write a memory level question on a piece of paper. The papers are handed to the student on the left. Using the same paper, each person writes a new question on the topic on the next higher level (translation). The papers are passed to the left and the third level question on the topic is written on the paper. When the papers are returned to their originators, there will be seven questions, one on each level. Now the group critiques each question by determining if it is reasonable and on the appropriate level.

Sanders' Question Levels	*Sample Teacher Prepared Questions*
1. *Rote or Memory* Question involving simple recall of facts.	1. Would you spell "que nada"?
2. *Translation* Question involving a request to change the form of facts.	2. What does "que nada" mean in English?
3. *Interpretation* Here the student is asked to explain a fact, usage or situation.	3. What did Jose mean when he used "que nada" in the paragraph on page 4?
4. *Application* Here the student applies the fact under discussion.	4. Can you write grammatically correct sentences using "que nada" in at least three ways? (Grading to be on proper application of grammar.)
5. *Analysis* Here the student is asked to make a judgement based upon existing criteria he did not determine.	5. Is the usage of "que nada" on page 7 correct?

Sanders' Question Levels	*Sample Teacher Prepared Questions*
6. *Synthesis* Here the student creates something original.	6. Can you write a poem which uses "que nada" at least twice? (Grading to be on student creativity, not on mere grammar.)
7. *Evaluation* Here the student makes a judgement, but unlike analysis he forms his own criteria.	7. Can you evaluate the popular song "Que Nada" to determine whether you like the way the term was used? Why do you feel that way?

The Teacher As Message Sender

The preceeding activities have been designed to build your skill in communicating with students. The point is dual: you *need* the skill to perform and you need to *know* that you have the skill in order to accept yourself and become confident. This process is just begun. As you proceed through the rest of the text, through your student teaching, and into your novice teaching, you should continue to sharpen your skills. Try to observe yourself via audio and video recording to see if you are practicing the skills presented here and, if not, practice upgrading your questioning practices. Only by using questions to invite students into the process can you begin to communicate with them.

Feedback from Students

Communication is a two-way process. As you teach, students will be sending both verbal and nonverbal messages. Be sure to work on the interpretation of these messages; they are sometimes hidden and do not always mean what they seem.

The importance of hidden messages can best be given by an example. The scene is an eighth grade social studies class. Students have each been given the assignment of labeling a map of Europe with country names, capitals, and other principal features. There are ten minutes left in the period. As the students begin to work, the teacher moves around the room checking on individual progress.

Near the front of the room, Ms. Jones stops at Ruth's desk. Ruth is eagerly following directions and is labeling the map correctly. Ms. Jones gives a quiet word of praise and moves on. (Diagnosis: Ruth is pursuing a *task event.* She understood the assignment and is getting it done. She is learning whatever one learns from map labeling. No problem here.)

As Ms. Jones arrives at Jane's desk, she sees that Jane is coloring the map.

"Jane, what are you doing?"

"Why, Ms. Jones," Jane explains, "this map will look so much better if I color it first and then label it."

"That's nice, Jane."

But what Ms. Jones did not see was that Jane did not really know how to do the assignment and knew that if she made a good show for only ten minutes, she could call Ruth for help at home. Jane does not want Ms. Jones to know that she does not know what to do. (Diagnosis: Jane is pursuing an *institutional event.* She is interested in survival in the institution and not in learning the task at hand. Teachers often mistake this kind of behavior for task behavior.)

Finally, Ms. Jones arrives at Robert's desk. He is drawing a hot rod.

"Robert, is it going to be another one of those days?"

"But, Ms. Jones, I didn't know what to do."

"You should have paid attention." (Diagnosis: Robert is pursuing a *personal event.* He may not know Jane's institutional method, or he may not care.)

In the process of communicating with students, you need to be aware of the hidden meanings in your feedback from the students. There will be at least three kinds of student events going on in your class. (There is a fourth: mixed events involving a blend of the other three.)

You will not have trouble with task events. You can identify students doing the right thing who merely need support and reinforcement.

You can spot students pursuing personal events as Robert did in the example. You need to remember that such behavior reflects a need for help, and you will have to invest time finding out why the Roberts are not working and what you should do to help.

The institutional events take longer to spot, but eventually you will be able to identify these students. They need help as much as the Roberts; however, they have become more successful in hiding their problems.

Problem 15

(Observation Activity: Teams of Two)

TASK, INSTITUTIONAL, PERSONAL STUDENT EVENTS

Observe a classroom or a film or videotape of a class with another education student. Try to identify one or two students in each of the previous categories and determine why they were pursuing their own event. Compare notes with your partner.

Hidden Meanings

In the American culture, it is not uncommon for people, including students and teachers, to avoid saying and doing what they really feel and mean. It becomes necessary to look occasionally for hidden meanings in classroom communication. This must not become an obsession, but it can help if you occasionally examine why your students say and do certain things. The task, institutional, and personal event framework just presented can help here.

Since all communication events have a nonverbal dimension and some are exclusively nonverbal, this area deserves special mention. It is not possible, in a methods text, to give this area the treatment it deserves. If you are interested in pursuing the topic further, you can use the bibliography at the end of the chapter.

These are certain principles in nonverbal communication that can be presented here.

1. *Congruence between the verbal and nonverbal dimensions is necessary to be credible.* As a teacher, your expression must match your words in order for students to believe what you are saying. This is where students catch teacher insincerity and fear.

2. *The nonverbal dimension is more open and honest than the verbal, so people often depend upon the nonverbal message.* Would you believe a student who says he is interested when he appears to be bored?

The effective teacher is the congruent teacher, the person with verbal-nonverbal congruence and no hidden meanings. Therefore, be genuine!

As a teacher, you will be able to use this knowledge to your advantage. Many of the students' hidden meanings can be seen rather than heard, even while you are lecturing. Few students will tell you to quit lecturing verbally, but they will send all kinds of nonverbal signals that mean the same: sleeping, restlessness, looking out the window, and so on.

How do you pick up skills in these sensitive areas? By observing others and by looking at yourself, preferably with media assistance. Videotape is best, but you will be surprised at what you can learn from audio tape or by having a partner observe you.

Readings on Nonverbal Communication

1. David K. Berlo, *The Process of Communication* (New York: Holt, Rinehart and Winston, 1960).
2. Eric Berne, *Games People Play* (New York: Grove Press, 1964).
3. Helen H. Davidson and Gerhard Lang, "Children's Perception of Their Teachers' Feelings Toward Them Related to Self-Perception, School Achievement and Behavior," *Journal of Experimental Education* 29 (December 1960), pp. 107–18.
4. Joel R. Davitz, *The Communication of Emotional Meanings* (New York: McGraw-Hill Book Company, 1964).
5. Charles M. Galloway, "Nonverbal Communication," *The Instructor* 77, no. 8 (April 1968), pp. 37–42.
6. Charles M. Galloway, "Nonverbal Communication," *Theory Into Practice* 7, no. 5 (December 1968), pp. 172–75.
7. Charles M. Galloway, "Teacher Nonverbal Communication," *Educational Leadership* 24 (October 1966), pp. 55–63.
8. Erving Goffman, *The Presentation of Self in Everyday Life* (Garden City, N.Y.: Doubleday, 1959).
9. Edward T. Hall, "Listening Behavior: Some Cultural Differences," *Phi Delta Kappan* 50, no. 7 (May 1969), pp. 379–80.
10. Herbert K. Heger, "Analyzing Verbal and Nonverbal Classroom Communications," Unpublished paper. Columbus: The Ohio State University, Summer 1968 (Abstracted in *Research in Education,* May 1969).

4

Focus on the Student

The Need to Reach the Student

The Frances Fuller study, referred to early in this book, indicates that young teachers are very concerned about their ability to survive and do well as a teacher. At this point in your career, you are probably most concerned about doing well as a teacher. This is very natural and derives from correct motives. You are likely to think along these lines: "If I do not do well and if I fail to control my class, I cannot contribute to the profession. I might as well give up if I cannot survive."

The dilemma is that *no* teacher can be effective unless he reaches the students. If the students are confused, unsuccessful, or dissatisfied with their class, they are likely to become uninterested, defensive, or even offensive.

Your professor understands this dilemma and probably has talked a great deal about reaching the students. You cannot survive unless you break out of your own survival concerns and reach the individuals in your classes. The content and activities in the previous section of this text were aimed at beginning to give you the communication skills you will need in reaching the students.

This section deals with the question of what it takes to involve students successfully and lays the groundwork for subsequent development of better ways to approach instruction.

Principle One: Student behavior provides you with specific data on what the students' motivations and interests are.

The teacher who fails to observe his students *while* he is teaching cannot accurately predict the next proper move. The teacher who fails to observe his class is likely to blindly stick to his lesson plan well beyond the point of lesson breakdown. If you have the courage to watch your students, you will know much earlier than this if your plan is failing. If that happens, you will face great pressure and it will take even greater courage to open up new approaches. Most students will be sympathetic to the teacher who dares to abandon unworkable plans; they will not sympathize with the person who just keeps doing the same old thing.

Principle Two: Your best approach is to attempt to interest your students rather than to try to motivate them.

Motivation and interest are not the same things. This point has caused massive confusion. Motivation refers to an inner drive that has been established over a long period. Interest is a short-term phenomenon which can be extrinsically stimulated.[1] You can interest students, but you cannot change their motivations in time to teach them. If you do your job well, you will find a long-term improvement in motivation and your students will thank you for their future success. But, daily teaching strategy must be built on interest and involvement, not motivation.

Principle Three: Some teaching methods are better than others in the area of generating student interest and involvement.

This principle will be developed throughout the remainder of this text. In general, you will observe that lectures do not work and that involvement strategies do help students and teachers.

One Project on Student Involvement

During the Summer of 1970, a group of thirty Neighborhood Youth Corps personnel worked at the University of Kentucky College of Education as Student Critics.[2] These disadvantaged high school students were potential drop outs. Most, but not all, of these students were black; some were lower-class white. Nearly all of these teenagers were very bright, although a few had not mastered certain basic skills such as reading. Their academic potential was much greater than actual performance, a common situation with inner-city students.

The NYC students took part in a college-wide program which provided education majors with various kinds of controlled direct experience. Guidance majors learned to counsel, in-service teachers improved their techniques and pre-service teachers observed and participated in a variety of micro-teaching experiences. The results of the summer program were viewed as highly successful in spite of some problems with hall noise and faculty tempers.

In one portion of this program, pre-service teachers who planned to student-teach during the fall after taking a general secondary methods course taught small groups of NYC students for one hour a week for seven weeks. Thirty of these pre-service teachers reported on the teaching strategy they tried and the duration of the attention span of their student-critics. Student interest in specific topics was also reported.

Lecture, as an instructional strategy, was a distinct failure. After a period of about five minutes, NYC students began to pursue other activities no matter what the student teacher did. If the topic was of personal interest, these teenagers would pay attention

---

[1]The research of Jack R. Frymier and Phillip Clark in the Center for the Study of Motivation and Human Abilities at the Ohio State University is important here. Their periodical *Motivation Quarterly* is a useful source of data.

[2]This study was conducted by the author.

for about ten minutes before they departed mentally, and in some cases physically. Even when they were concerned with the topic, these students could not become interested in lectures.

Lectures which followed open discussion of a topic were more successful. It seemed that once a teacher had listened to their views, the students then wanted to hear the teacher. This seemed to be true regardless of the kind of lecture, summary, or new content presentation. The attention span was often twenty minutes for this kind of lecture.

These teenagers loved to talk and would do so as long as the teacher permitted it. Bull sessions would last an hour. Guided discussion which remained on the topic and which achieved closure would hold their attention for about 45 minutes, a respectable span.

The use of visual aids did not help lectures very much, although question and answer techniques about features of a visual aid seemed to work for about twenty minutes. However, visual aides were generally a disappointment for the pre-service teachers. Perhaps poor AV aids had been over-used in the public school experience of these young people. In fact, they would make many negative comments about the cosmetic quality of the AV materials. Movies were unmercifully attacked as "crummy" and "tacky." They seemed to demand the Walt Disney level of production quality for AV aids.

Question and answer techniques worked well with the NYC students. They all seemed ready and willing to play along with a student teacher as long as this conventional means of involving students was pursued.

Skits were a disaster. These teenagers did not want to stand in front of a class and reveal themselves. By contrast, role play which involved all students was a great success. No timidity was revealed in role play. In fact, the students were very enthusiastic about all innovative teaching methods, especially role playing, simulation, and gaming.

Inner-city students seemed to be interested in any topic of personal experience. Nutrition, health, sex, housing, community planning, police, and similar topics were readily discussed. There were, however, some surprises. Black history was a bust. The students wanted to know about the here and now in the city. The past was dead to them and African topics were just irrelevant.

Space programs were rejected as a topic because the students saw them as detracting from the solution of urban troubles. But certain teachers could discuss poetry with AV aids and hold their attention. Perhaps it was the image of a better life that motivated this concern.

Art was a successful area for instruction as long as the students were actively involved in the production of art.

The results of this project indicate that students from the inner city need active involvement. They are much more group encapsulated than a white teacher suspects. They have not developed an interest in areas outside of their own experience and they are worried about being victims of violence. *Instructional strategies based upon active involvement of students and which capitalize on personal experience work well with inner-city teenagers.*

Summary of Teaching Techniques Effective
With Inner City Students

Technique	Attention Span*
Formal lecture	5 minutes
Formal lecture on topic of personal interest	10 minutes
Directions and activities, alternating	45 minutes
Movies	10 to 30 minutes
Movies on space programs	0 minutes
AV aids with questions and answers during presentation	20 minutes
Questions and answers, no AV aids	5 minutes
Art work: drawing, collage making, etc.	45 minutes
Art lecture (illustrated after several art lessons)	20 to 30 minutes
Lectures after discussion	10 to 20 minutes
Viewing self on video	20 minutes
Games	45 minutes
Role play on topic of personal experience	45 minutes
Skits	0 to 20 minutes
Open discussion	45 minutes
Guided discussion	30 to 45 minutes
Discussion of topic beyond personal experience	0 minutes
Literature discussion—illustrated	45 minutes

Productive topics: cities, environment, health, social issues
Unproductive topics: literature, space, physics

*Mean observed class attention span with groups of 16 NYC student critics.

Problem 16

The following activities are designed to drive home some points about how students feel in typical and innovative classes.

16–1. (Individual)

LECTURE VICTIM ACTIVITY

This activity is intended to establish a need to master teaching methods other than lecture. Since you are currently a student, it should still be relatively easy for you to document the ineffectiveness of lecture as a teaching method.

As you pursue this activity, remember that the students you are observing are able but that as a high school teacher you must reach all students, not just the able.

Step 1. Observe students in three of your college classes. Record your estimate of the percentage of students still listening to the lecture at the designated time intervals.

	Class 1	Class 2	Class 3
10 minutes			
20 minutes			
30 minutes			
40 minutes			

Step 2. Write a paragraph on how you would expect these figures to change for high school students of *average* ability. You may wish to refer to the NYC data discussed earlier in this section.

16–2. (Discussion Groups of Four to Six)

Discuss in groups the significance of your data and the relative potential of lecturing. *What is it like to be a student in a lecture?*

16–3. (Entire Class)

MODIFIED COUNTRY "X" SIMULATION

You have a reasonable notion of what it is like to be a student in a lecture. The next activity will contrast that feeling with a perception of what it is like to be a student in a lesson conducted very differently, by simulation. You will return to the simulation presented here for experiences with the teacher's side of the teaching-learning process. At the moment, the focus is on the student.

Your professor will divide your class into groups of five or six persons each. Your task is to role play the part of high school students and then to analyze the results of the experience and its implications for your own teaching. It should be emphasized that this activity is limited to one class period to establish the feel of participating actively in the learning process and that the same package used in a regular classroom would be longer and more detailed to insure content development.

Directions: 1. Appoint a recording secretary.
2. Examine the five maps of Country X on pages 194 through 198 Notice that the country is essentially virgin with only one settlement at X on the mouth of river A. You have all essential geographic data about the area on the five maps. Special note should be taken of the large area involved, nearly continental in size.
3. In about fifteen minutes you are to project the locations of three new settlements that will be created by the residents of city X as they outgrow their first town. Be certain to base these locations on the principle that the migrating people would like to preserve their life styles. Therefore, determine the kind of livelihood the people in town X pursue and use that as a basis for locating new settlements. Have the recording secretary make notes on the sites selected and the reasons for these selections.
4. Return to the large group and compare notes on the results of the small group projections. The discussion should focus on:
   a. A report by the group secretary on how the sites were selected and the reasons for the selections.
   b. The nature of the different choices made by the groups and whether these results were based upon different assumptions about the residents of town X or different interpretations of the map data.
   c. What kinds of judgements can be made about the accuracy of these projections?
5. Return to your small groups and discuss your perceptions of the effect of participating in simulations versus listening to a lecture on territorial expansion.
6. Individually, prepare a summation on your position on content development via simulation versus lecturing to be submitted to your instructor.

16–4.   *(Task Groups of 3)*

If you are like most students, you probably enjoyed participating in "Country X" more than you would have enjoyed an average lecture. How do your responses and feelings compare with those of a high school student? You have certainly read how high school students respond to instruction, you have heard lectures on the topic, and you have participated in discussions on how to reach these students. But, in concrete terms, can you identify with their perceptions of classroom activities? Perhaps a comparison activity will help.

Step 1. Briefly discuss your perceptions, as a group, of the typical lecture. What is it like to be a student in a lecture? What degree of mental involvement is induced by a lecture? Is your mental involvement a product of the professor's lecture or your own academic drives?

Step 2. As college students, you attend classes about fifteen hours a week. What would happen to your mental involvement in lectures if you had to sit through twenty-five hours of lecture a week? In your brief discussion, assume you had to attend all classes or the campus police would come looking for you.

Step 3. You probably concluded that you would have greater difficulty remaining mentally involved in lectures if you attended class for a longer period. The example given matches the high school students' situation. He must attend class six hours a day, and most of these classes are variations on lectures. Thus far you have been discussing college student's perceptions of the lecture, but high school students represent a broader range of abilities than college students. Discuss how you think high school student reactions would compare with yours.

Step 4. Let's go back to the lecture form again and make a different point. In your freshman year, you had academic experiences that made a positive, lasting impression. Try to remember them and list them. (Note: by academic experience, the author means any experience which assisted your learning a subject. Examples would be lectures, in-class discussions, private sessions with instructors, dormitory study sessions, and open discussions at the pub.)

Step 5. The principle being developed here is that students have greater retention of
learning experiences in which their involvement went beyond merely thinking
about what the instructor says. Where the student can also talk, he tends to
become more involved and learn more. Is this true? Write a paragraph on the
principle of student involvement.

Observations About Involving Students

The greater the degree of student involvement,
the greater the degree of retention.

This point has been reasonably well established by now. It should be noted here that
for most forms of instruction, mental involvement is the key. However, greater physical
involvement accentuates mental involvement. The teacher who has students *doing*
things is likely to be more effective than the instructor who requires students to listen,
provided that the physical involvement is on the topic at hand.

Students will often participate in learning activities
when they would not listen to the same data in traditional form.

It is true that activity relieves boredom; doing something is always better than just
sitting and listening. But the principles of involvement are stronger than merely
eliminating boredom. Students are peer oriented. They will become interested in things
their friends find interesting, where they might find the teacher's interest in the subject
uninspiring. As you get ready to teach, it is important to remember that students,

especially teenage students, are highly peer oriented, and they will do things for and with their peers they will not do for or with you.

Of course you are wondering how student involvement affects you as a new teacher. Greater student involvement assists in reducing your problems in controlling your class since the students are more nearly pursuing things of interest to them and to their peers than they would be if you lectured.

As you involve students, your role changes. As a lecturer, you must give data and control the class at the same time. In forms of instruction that involve students, the instructor assumes a new, less strenuous role. In "Country X" and in many of the other activities of this text you may have noticed that your instructor's role was more relaxed than when he lectures. In these several activities he helped the class organize and start the task, and then he observed and offered advice and assistance from time to time. If you utilize methods of involving students in your instruction, you will find that your role will be more relaxed and you will be able to learn about your students and offer them more precise help than if you merely lecture at them.

Olson's study which was examined earlier shows that teachers fail to involve their students, and your personal experience is likely to confirm this. We need to determine what keeps experienced teachers from taking advantage of student involvement. More importantly, how can you avoid the same trap?

Some teachers may not fully understand the weaknesses of the present lecture-oriented methods. The author's hope is that you have some understanding at this point of the need to break new ground in instructional methods.

Some teachers have problems in selecting strategies of teaching which match the objectives of their intended lesson, and they have trouble selecting varying format patterns over a period of time. The next chapter will address this problem and you will be given a mechanism to use which will enable you to match the function of each lesson to the appropriate strategy and a method of looking at a unit of instruction so that the variety or lack of variety in your instructional plans becomes clear.

Some teachers have not had experience with instructional alternatives, and many student teachers are limited to the existing methods in their student teaching. To some extent, you have now had experience from the student viewpoint with certain alternative methods in gaming, simulation, and small group work as a result of this text. A later chapter will focus on these methods from the instructor's viewpoint so that you may gain experience with significant new methods of instruction.

5

Planning and
Teaching Strategies

Our Approach and Its Limitations

By now you should have some convictions about the need to teach differently, and you are aware of the dangers of merely imitating other teachers. You understand the advantages of developing lesson plans that effectively involve students. You probably see the need to interest students and the companion need to avoid excessive lecturing. You have seen hints of better ways to teach in the "Socratic Teaching Game" and in "Country X" and must now be asking the classic question: "Just how do I accomplish all of this?" Here and in the next chapter you will begin the task of developing specific ideas about ways to teach.

The focus of these two chapters is specific. You need specific data to become confident of your own teaching abilities. There are dangers in this approach. You might interpret the specific teaching methods developed herein as recipes to be automatically applied without thought or effort. Nothing could be further from the truth. *All specifics* developed in this text *must be modified* according to the environment in which you use them.

A natural tendency of teachers is to prepare a lesson plan which is essentially script-like. The specific nature of the strategies developed here could make it appear that lesson planning is little more than script writing. Actually, master teachers go into class with a series of prepared alternatives which make it possible to change the entire direction of their lesson if the need arises. *Planning must be flexible.*

A final danger of the specific approach taken here is that you might think of this text and the methods course you are now taking as more complete than they possibly can be. Your course and this text are merely launching devices to get you ready for micro-teaching, student teaching, and the first phase of your professional career. Unlike a course in Greek history, which provides closure (a sense of completion) for the student, methods courses expose new horizons. Nothing developed here represents a final answer; rather, it represents possible first steps you may take to become a professional teacher.

The focus of these two chapters is on practical strategies of teaching rather than upon systems of instruction. The focus is on methods you can use in your classroom rather than upon systems which require outside help, such as school reorganization or special media. The focus is on the practical rather than on the ideal.

Teaching strategies, teaching methods, and teaching techniques are nearly synonymous for our purposes. They all refer to specific ways of teaching a class that you may choose without special help from outside your classroom. Some people confuse these terms with systems of instruction. Unlike specific strategies of instruction, systems of instruction represent families of instructional strategies assembled in a specific, systematic manner. CAI, computer-assisted instruction, is an example of a system of instruction which includes a series of strategies. It also happens to be media assisted. II, individualized instruction, is another instructional system which includes a multitude of strategies within it.

Instructional systems are not rare in American education. However, they usually require reorganization of the school and intensive teacher retraining in the use of the specific system. You should know that such changes are becoming common and you have the right to expect expert help at the time you become involved in new systems. At this point, however, we are concerned with first steps, with a focus on specific teaching strategies and how to organize them into segments or units of instruction.

Some Assumptions About the Nature of Teaching

As a novice, you probably hope to get answers to your very specific questions about how to teach. You probably have found that professors of education often have a difficult time becoming specific. There is a very valid reason for this; educators are not really in agreement about the basic purpose of teaching and about the role of the teacher.

Some people argue that the teacher and the school have no right to control the student's development. In this view, the teacher is rather like a librarian leading the student to whatever answers he wants to know. At *no time* would the teacher teach or preach in the usual sense; he would never carry an intent to lessons.

By contrast, some people argue that all school experiences exist to insure the continuation of society and that *society dictates* what the teacher must do. In this view, the teacher fosters conventional democratic values and academic goals. The school is teacher-controlled, not student-controlled.

One cannot resolve the question of what to do until one resolves the question of goals and purposes. Some professions do not have this kind of problem. For example, in medicine there is general agreement on the need to preserve the health of the client by preventative and remedial methods. The arguments and crises in medicine are over how to best reach the goal. In education, we are still fighting over the nature of the goal.

Until the goals of education are defined, the only course open to the teacher-educator is to make some assumptions about the nature and purpose of teaching and to build his recommendations about specific ways to teach on these assumptions. This path creates the need to identify assumptions used so that the relevance of methods developed is subject to examination.

The assumptions made by this author are that teaching is an *intentional process* requiring considerable teacher control of the situation, but that student freedom to inquire and explore is one of the teacher's major intents. Student freedom needs to be planned in order to prevent anarchy. There are certain academic and social goals of teaching which are non-negotiable: *every student* should be taught the dignity of man; all students need certain academic and social skills, and so on.

The teacher must also plan to assist the student develop self-realization and self-control. This requires that the teacher plan for periods of time in which the student controls his own activities and the teacher merely guides. This open portion of the curriculum should increase as the student matures and may reach as high as 60 percent of the school day in high school. However, the teacher will always be expected to *lead* because he is more mature and more familiar with the topics and tasks of the classroom.

The strategies of instruction developed here are based upon an essentially middle-of-the-road position concerning dual needs: *the teacher must intend to teach and the student must have freedom to grow.*

Planning for Instruction

You should never enter the classroom without a specific plan for action. This plan of action should be very unlike traditional lesson plans. It should not be a script, but instead a series of alternatives designed to reach an objective. The plan should anticipate failures and breakdowns in lessons. It should encourage you to do something other than give speeches.

The Syllabus

The odds are about 999 to 1 that you will be presented with a syllabus as you receive your teaching assignment. Most teachers blindly follow the syllabus and text. You are likely to be tempted to do the same. The odds are that you will not have the time or energy to make a new syllabus, but will be limited to modifying it. Therefore, planning for instruction will be presented as *looking beyond* the syllabus.

The syllabus is a very limited document. Written by a committee of teachers, it is usually limited to a series of notes about topics to be covered in a course. It gives few ideas about how to teach. It is usually weak on goals and objectives. You can expect little help on why the students should do what the syllabus requires. The syllabus is usually too limited to help you, and in fact, the only people the syllabus helps are those who wrote it.

The syllabus is intended to encourage planning of large segments of instruction and to eliminate chaotic day-by-day planning. The syllabus can help with content identification and in locating teaching materials. Look at your syllabus as a starting point in your planning process.

Problem 17

Teams of Two or Three

Your task is to determine the ways in which a syllabus can help a teacher as well as to find the limits of a syllabus as a resource. Analyze a two-week section of a syllabus in your discipline. Evaluate the data in the syllabus as determined by the criteria listed below. You will find sample syllabi in your college curriculum materials center or in the local schools. Give your analysis to your instructor. He will return it for use in Problem 19.

1. Purposes, goals, objectives:

2. Concepts, principles:

3. Facts, skills:

4. Process dimension of content:

5. Student learning style:

6. Ways to vary content:

7. Ways to vary pace:

8. Ways to vary teaching strategy:

9. Data on sources of materials for teaching:

   As a source of planning assistance, most syllabi are limited to topical outlines, lists of activities, and sources of materials. They provide some indication of relative importance of topics by means of time allotments. Incidentally, time allotments are indicators of relative importance, not rigid scheduling mandates. Seldom will a class progress at the rate indicated in the master plan. You are likely to need to replan time factors in terms of class progress and topical importance.

Much of your planning will be based upon the syllabus, but you will need to consider factors not included in it. The point made by Problem 17 is that many factors are not available in the usual syllabus. The planning task is to move beyond the syllabus to include missing elements. Before dealing with other elements, it may help to review planning hurdles you will face.

Hurdle One: Curriculum Planning in Isolation

As a new teacher, you will receive little help in curriculum. You will work in isolation with few contacts with fellow teachers. It will be very difficult for you to uncover the large picture and to discover how the curricular pieces fit together. As there is more to teaching than recitation of content, so there is more to planning than dealing with fragments of content.

An example of the kind of problem that can arise from Hurdle One occurred to this author several years ago. Formal logic was included in an algebra class. When the class reached this topic, there was a general class breakdown. Students begun asking questions such as, "This logic is so different than English logic; why do we have to learn two kinds of logic?" Upon investigation, the author discovered that English and mathematics teachers were teaching the same logic without any coordination whatsoever. They taught logic at different times and used different symbolism for identical concepts. The texts in English and mathematics had been selected without consideration of the common topic. The crisis, in this instance, was resolved after several classes of students had been needlessly confused.

As you begin to teach, make every effort to review the total curriculum. Look for areas of overlap and potential conflict. Try to correct those weaknesses in your planning.

Hurdle Two: Understanding the Nature of Disciplines

Overcoming Hurdle One cannot be accomplished without overcoming Hurdle Two. You need to develop an understanding of the nature of your own discipline, of the other disciplines, and how they relate. This is exceedingly difficult. You probably have not had any academic experience in other areas. Yet, interdisciplinary curricular efforts are underway which are likely to affect you as a teacher. This topic is worthy of a course or two; however, we will have to make do with an example to demonstrate its nature.

Suppose a medical doctor, a psychologist, a sociologist, and a political scientist were waiting at a corner to cross a street when a pretty young girl walked by. What would they see? Yes, they would see some of the same things as a plumber driving by in his truck. As members of the human race, they would make judgements about what kind of person she is, such as pretty or ugly. To some extent all observers could cross the boundaries of their specialty. After all, even a layman can recognize beauty. The point of this example is: what would they see in terms of their disciplines? All disciplines represented on this corner deal with the human condition in one way or another. The political scientist is likely to think about how the girl fits into the large-scale patterns of human decision making, politics. The sociologist would take a more limited view in terms of sub-groups of society and how the girl would fit into one group. The psychologist would take an even more limited view and would observe how the girl behaves in her environment. The doctor's concern is even more limited to biological processes and her physical health. The perspective and concern taken by each person is different. Yet, if you want to know all about this girl, you describe her from all of these vantage points in addition to other disciplinary viewpoints not included here.

Inter-disciplinary relationships are important. Mathematics, by itself, is limited in use, but in a social context it has great importance and is related to other disciplines. It has utility and is used in most other disciplines; it also has great beauty and is fundamental to art and music. Mathematics appreciation must be done in context.

Hurdle Three: Avoiding Unneeded Facts

Facts are too often the heart of academic programs. Yet facts can be transitory. As our knowledge expands, the facts change and our interpretation of stable facts and their implications changes. In planning instruction, you need to go beyond facts to the concepts, principles, and processes underlying them. There is no point in a student memorizing the Periodic Table in a chemistry class. He can always look it up. It might even change through the addition of newly discovered elements. Hence, it is more important to understand the concepts behind the table and the general relationships between elements. You need to be careful to assure that all facts you teach illuminate something more important, such as a concept or process.

Hurdle Four: Relevance

This hurdle is a difficult barrier to good teaching. Teachers often know things that will be important to students, but the students are not yet aware of the importance.

This hurdle requires that you identify student concerns and interests and build from them toward the content you know to be vital. This process is difficult and far slower than merely presenting facts, but it is a vital process if you want to produce results. It cannot be taught in a methods course and takes time to master. You need to become skeptical of syllabi since they seldom reflect this kind of sophistication. You need to begin to observe and analyze students so you can base your future plans on real needs.

There are more hurdles to good planning than have been discussed here. The point has been simply to establish the need to plan and to indicate the nature of the planning resources you will have on hand in your classroom.

Three Major Lesson Purposes

The stages of instruction are the same whether applied to a unit of instruction of a week or longer or to a single class period. The teacher needs introductory lessons to get the unit started, developmental lessons as a means of helping the student reach the objective, and wrap-up lessons to complete the unit in a cohesive manner. In each lesson, the same three stages are found. These stages need to be included in planning for entire courses as well as for units and lessons.

Teachers generally understand the need to introduce the day's activities as the lesson starts and to bring some kind of conclusion at the end of the lesson. They also understand this need in relation to a year's work, but not in relation to smaller units of instruction. One result of this situation is that too many teachers fail to ascertain that students understand and are interested in what is going on. Most class time seems to be devoted to content development and little to the other two main lesson purposes.

Lesson Purpose One: To Establish Instructional Set

Lessons intended to develop "instructional set" are best described as those which introduce a topic *and* develop student intent to learn about it. These lessons are far more than the usual introductions. In a concrete way, they face up to the question, "Why bother to learn this stuff?" and work on the problem until the student determines to study. This is a vital stage in the development of the topic you intend to teach, and you cannot teach until the student intends to learn.

Instructional set lessons fulfill the following purposes:

1. Introducing the topic.
2. Establishing the importance of the topic.
3. Generating student interest in the topic and creating an intent to learn.
4. Establishing goals and objectives for the unit.
5. Delimiting scope of topic and activities.
6. Establishing the central points of the lesson to come and a mechanising of the sorting of the important from the unimportant topics, facts, concepts, principles.
7. Diagnosis of student needs.

Instructional set lessons are more than introductions, so much more that failure to spend enough time and energy on instructional set will defeat all subsequent lessons. The teaching strategies used in these lessons are not always like the methods used in other types of lessons.

Lesson Purpose Two: To Provide Developmental Experiences

These lessons are probably more familiar to you. Developmental Experiences include factual development, skill development, and so on. These are the lessons which cover the heart of the topic in a content sense.

Lesson Purpose Three: To Provide Closure

Closure is the wrap-up stage of instruction, but it is more than mere summary. Closure implies strong reinforcement of the learning which has occurred and the establishment of a sense of completion and accomplishment on the part of the student. Evaluation of student achievement also fits into the closure stage of instruction. Relating the completed topic to other topics is as vital here as it was in instructional set.

Lesson Sequencing

It should be obvious that the sequence of lessons will always run from instructional set through developmental experiences to closure, yet the implications of this sequence need to be clarified.

A Typical Sequence of Lessons
Topic: Quadratic Equations

Lesson 1	The origins and history of quadratic equations.
Lesson 2	The philosophic assumptions behind quadratics.
Lesson 3	The theoretical framework of quadratics.
Lesson 4	The generalized form of quadratics.
Lesson 5	How to solve quadratics.
Lesson 6-9	Practice in solving quadratics.
Lesson 10	Test.

The example may seem overstated, but it represents the tendency many teachers have when dealing with able students. For less able students, these same teachers omit lessons one through three to simplify things. Either way, there is a complete failure to deal with instructional set. At no point does the student find out why he should bother with quadratics.

What is needed in this example is a strong instructional set and a reorganization of topics with the more theoretical and abstract items at the end of the sequence. The question, "Why bother?" demands a series of concrete experiences and a postponement of the abstract until the student is well along toward mastery of the quadratic solution process and begins to wonder about why quadratics are like they are or how they fit into the larger scheme of mathematics.[1]

Problem 18

Same Teams as in Problem 17

BUILDING A UNIT PLAN

1. Your task is to try long-range planning and to develop a set of general planning notes. Base your effort on the syllabus and notes from Problem 17.

---

[1]Hilda Taba, *Curriculum Development: Theory and Practice* (New York: Harcourt, Brace and World, 1962).

One solution to the planning problem you will face is to enrich the syllabus. Your aim should be a clarified syllabus which includes data on three key areas not usually included in syllabi.

1. Notes on the concepts, principles, and processes which are the real objectives behind the topics in the syllabus.
2. Notes on data sources and visual aides to be used in instruction.
3. Plans for a few highly selected key activities for students.

Do not try to write a master plan or script. Rather, you should develop the basic importance of the unit, a better list of content sources for the segment of instruction, and a limited number of keystone activites which will highlight the section. (The suggested form below should help you organize your plan.) Remember that this is a general plan, not a lesson plan, so there is no need to develop specific teaching strategies at this point.

The specifications of your plan should include the following:

1. Concrete to abstract organization
2. Lessons dealing with instructional set
3. Lessons providing developmental experiences
4. Lessons providing closure
5. A general tone which would interest students

Unit Plan

Subject _____ Grade Level ___ Topic _____

Main Concepts, Principles or Processes   Student Objectives

1. _____   1. _____
2. _____   2. _____
3. _____   3. _____

No. of classes	Topic	Major points of topic	Major student activity	What student will be able to do at end

Final Outcomes: How student
                                                                       will relate
                                                                       this topic to
                                                                       his other
                                                                       experiences

Note: Use 8½" x 11" paper sideways. List on another page material and AV sources for this plan.

2. Give your plan to another team and have them evaluate it according to the criteria in Problem 17 and the specifications above. The question is how your plan improves upon the syllabus. They will return your plan and give you written comments.

3. Revise your plan if necessary. Write a few paragraphs explaining how it will (a) meet student needs, (b) convey really important concepts, and (c) hold student interest through variety. Submit the plan and paper to your instructor.

Strategies of Instruction

It has been well established that school is a dull and boring place for students. This situation is caused by the excessive monotony of instructional processes actually in use. Drill techniques are an example. Drill methods are based on the solid principle that active involvement is essential to the learning process. As long as students are actively working on the task at hand, they are more likely to learn than if they are just sitting around listening to a monotone lecture. The problem with drill is that it represents one of the very few ways teachers know how to get students involved, so they overuse the strategy. Even lecture has its place, but the problem is overuse of techniques.

It is, of course, true that all students differ in the precise ways in which they learn, and as a result the only long-range solution is true individualization of instruction. This requires a complete redesign of school operations and retraining of teachers; therefore, on the short term, you will have to make do with something less than a new system of school operation.

The near-term solution is to apply the following principles:

1. Always build your units with instructional set, developmental experiences, and closure, but be especially careful to establish a "need to know" on the part of your students before you start content development.
2. Base your instruction on active involvement of your students (up to 60 percent of the time).
3. Vary your day-to-day instructional strategies; do not fall into the trap of overusing your favorite methods.
4. Vary the size and structure of the class, utilize independent study and small group instruction.
5. Deal with the problem of student attention span (see data on page 142).

Your next step is to study teaching strategies and to practice selecting strategies to fit both the needs of the students and the topic at hand. The Teaching Strategy Selector which follows is presented to assist you in this process. You need to keep in mind that the activities which follow the Teaching Strategy Selector are somewhat hypothetical at this stage since you probably do not have direct contact with students at this point in your training.

	GROUP SIZE / LESSON PURPOSE	LARGE GROUP	SMALL GROUP	INDEPENDENT STUDY
INSTRUCTIONAL SET METHODS	MOTIVATION	LG2, LG4, LG5, LG6, LG9	SG2, SG3, SG4, SG5, SG7	I5, I6
	GOAL DEVELOPMENT	LG4, LG9	SG3, SG4, SG5, SG7	I6
	DEVELOPMENT STUDENT-STUDENT RAPPORT		SG1, SG2, SG3, SG4, SG5, SG7	
	DIAGNOSIS	LG4, Pretest	SG6,	I6 Interview
	INTRODUCTION	LG3, LG4, LG6, LG7, LG8, LG9	SG4, SG5, SG7	I4, I5
DEVELOPMENTAL METHODS	LEARNING FACTS	LG4, LG5, LG9	SG3, SG5, SG6, SG7	I1, I2, I4, I5
	RETAINING FACTS	LG4, LG5	SG2, SG5, SG6, SG7	I1, I2, I3, I4, I5
	PRINCIPLES/ CONCEPTS	LG4, LG5, LG7, LG8, LG9	SG3, SG5, SG6, SG7	I1, I2, I4, I5
	PROCEDURES	LG1, LG4, LG7, LG8	SG5, SG6, SG7	I2, I4
	SKILL DEVELOPMENT		SG2, SG3	I1, I2, I3, I6
	EXPRESSION DEVELOPMENT	LG4, LG5, LG9	SG2, SG5	I1, I2, I3, I6
	ATTITUDE/ OPINION DEVELOPMENT	LG4, LG8, LG9	SG5, SG7	I5
CLOSURE METHODS	SUMMARY-REVIEW	LG3, LG4, LG7, LG8, LG9	SG1, SG5, SG7	I2, I4, I6
	ASSESSMENT	LG4, LG5, Test	SG6	I2, I3, I4, I6

The Teaching Strategy Selector

The Teaching Strategy Selector is a directory which answers vital questions about the characteristics and potential uses of a group of teaching strategies. It can help the new teacher select the best method of presenting material, and data is included to assist him in determining the potential receptivity of students to the technique selected. This strategy list is designed to help you begin to build your own techniques. Space is provided at the end of the Selector for the addition of teaching strategies you may wish to add. *The list is not complete. Feel free to alter these methods.*

Directions

Determine the content of the lesson you wish to present. Then decide whether you wish to present the lesson in large group instruction, small group instruction, or independent study. Also determine the function of the lesson: learning facts, learning concepts, motivation, etc.; then examine the Teaching Strategy Selector on page 159. It will identify by number specific strategies which may suit your purposes. Read the description of each method and select the one you wish to try.

Example: You desire a small group lesson which assists in retaining facts. Look under the Small Group column on the Teaching Strategy Selector and on the Retaining Facts row. The strategy key numbers listed there lead you to the descriptions of several strategies from which you may choose. In this case, SG2, SG5, SG6, or SG7 are likely choices for you to use.

Notes on Sequencing Lessons

In general, all lesson sequences should procede from the top to the bottom on the Teaching Strategy Selector. Begin with a starting lesson, follow with a developmental series of lessons, and end with closure methods. Be careful to select a variety of methods in the three formats. Often large group lessons should be limited to 40 percent of class time. *Plan to shift formats* in your lesson sequence.

Once you have a sequence plan, do not become rigid. On occasion, you will need to return to instructional set approaches to give your students new direction. On occasion, you will need to prepare two or three alternatives for the same lesson in order to be able to shift to a new approach if a lesson fails to work.

LARGE GROUP STRATEGY 1

DIRECTION LECTURE

Definition: A direction-type lecture is a teacher presentation about how students are to do in a particular activity. The student role is confined to listening, note taking, and asking clarifying questions.

Current Use:	Moderate. This is one of the few ways to present directions. In some cases a live or media demonstration can also work.
Planning:	Presentation planning is very simple. Planning time should be spent on the details of the activities students will engage in.
Student Involvement:	Rather low in this presentation, but higher in the activity to follow.
Motivation:	Varies according to the student interest in and ability to do the planned activity. This lesson may reveal how well you planned the activity and on occasion you may need to change your plans. If such is the case, it is better to redesign the plan than to force it through the unwilling atmosphere.
Teacher Content Control:	Strong in this particular lesson.
Student Content Control:	Weak in this lesson.
Uses:	Limited to learning procedures.

LARGE GROUP STRATEGY 2

INSPIRATIONAL LECTURE

Definition:	Students listen while teachers gives them a sermon.
Current Use:	Few teachers are good at pep talks but most teachers do try to inspire frequently. Overuse in terms of teacher skills.
Planning:	Greater than you would expect. It takes great skill to prepare for a planned inspirational lecture and a different but equally complex skill to give impromptu pep talks.
Student Involvement:	Very low unless you are a Billy Graham.
Motivation:	Usually much lower than you would expect. Students tend to be defensive about why they are being subjected to these pep talks.
Teacher Content Control:	Maximum, for few students dare to interrupt a sermon.
Student Content Control:	Virtually none.
Uses:	Very few. Teachers often use this method to try to correct low motivation levels, failing to recognize the long-term nature of

motivation. Unless you have the talents of Billy Graham or some great new idea, forget this method.

LARGE GROUP STRATEGY 3

CONTENT LECTURE

Definition:	The teacher presents content in a logical order while the students listen, ask a few clarifying questions, and take notes.
Current Use:	Excessive. Teachers do this kind of thing because they don't know what else to do. Avoid it where possible and don't use it when you are confused about what to do.
Planning:	Presentation planning is relatively simple. Content is arranged in logical order. Care is necessary to anticipate the points at which questions will arise.
Student Involvement:	Relatively low for academically able students. For students without certain academic skills or without adequate motivation, involvement will be near zero.
Motivation:	This technique adds little to existing student motivation and if overused, can kill motivation. Motivation must come from sources other than this kind of lesson.
Teacher Content Control:	Very high unless students interrupt with questions.
Student Content Control:	Virtually none unless students wish to protest actively.
Uses:	The main characteristic of lecture is rapid content presentation. Therefore, use should be limited to situations where speed is more important than depth. Introduction of new topics and summaries or reviews can sometimes be done by lecture. Retention is low, so don't use lecture for in-depth topics.

LARGE GROUP STRATEGY 4

DISCUSSION

Definition:	Discussion is an open lesson in which the teacher leads the interaction toward a particular objective.
Current Use:	Moderate. This is one of the more effective techniques teachers currently use, although too many teachers permit discussions to become mere bull sessions.

Planning:	Moderately difficult. The main planning task is to build a series of questions leading to a conclusion and a collection of alternate questions for use in unplanned situations.
Student Involvement:	About optimum for a large group setting as long as the teacher actually involves all students.
Motivation:	Generally better than most large group methods.
Teacher Content Control:	Varies according to the planned freedom given the students, but is usually considerable.
Student Content Control:	Good, unless the teacher reverts to lecture or relies too heavily on one or two students.
Uses:	Quite varied. Examples are: development of content; analysis of student knowledge; group decision making; attitude and value development.

LARGE GROUP STRATEGY 5

PUPIL REPORT

Definition:	A lecture given by a student based upon his own research.
Current Use:	Moderate, although too many reports are usually given at one time.
Planning:	Simple for the actual presentation. Most of the planning is accomplished at the topic selection stage.
Student Involvement:	High for the reporter. If these reports are widely spaced, the involvement will be good for all students. When thirty reports are given back-to-back, involvement is weak.
Motivation:	High for able, self-confident students. Many students have a great fear of this kind of activity, so introduce it to them stage by stage and give them psychological support. On occasion, a student may prepare a good report and be unable to make the presentation. When this happens, do not press him. Perhaps having two-pupil report teams can help draw out the shy students. Don't criticize the students excessively.
Teacher Content Control:	Good through topic selection.
Student Content Control:	Fair if the teacher assigns the topic. Very good if the student and teacher negotiate the topic.
Uses:	Most types of content presentation. For the reporter, the uses are in the reinforcement and retention of content and, if properly handed, in the area of expression development.

LARGE GROUP STRATEGY 6

GUEST EXPERT

Definition:	A presentation by a guest, usually a lecture.
Current Use:	Infrequent, since it usually requires getting a volunteer from the community.
Planning:	Very difficult. Not only does the teacher have to find a willing party and schedule the lesson, but he has to prepare the guest in terms of the topic that is appropriate for his class.
Student Involvement:	Very little in the typical format, but may increase if discussion is permitted.
Motivation:	Varies widely according to the guest selected.
Teacher Content Control:	Very little once the lesson is underway. This makes planning especially vital.
Student Content Control:	Very little in guest lecture, more if other formats are used or if students helped select the guest.
Uses:	Motivation in and survey of a topic area. There are also some uses in establishing school-community rapport or student-establishment rapport.

LARGE GROUP STRATEGY 7

DEMONSTRATION

Definition:	A "how to do it" or "how it works" presentation by the teacher or a student. A form of illustrated direction giving; usually performed live although various media can be used.
Current Use:	Moderate. Teachers typically understand the strengths of demonstrations and apply them properly.
Planning:	Usually part of a planning sequence for a series of activities including the student assignments. The demonstration planning is usually fairly simple; however many teachers fail to assure that the students can adequately see the dynamic portion of the demonstration.
Student Involvement:	Fairly passive, unless aiding in the demonstration.
Motivation:	Directly related to the student motivation for the activity to follow in the case of a "how to do it" demonstration. In a "how it works" demonstration, motivation may be better than in a lecture, but not as high as when the students can try it themselves.

Teacher *Content Control:*	High.
Student *Content Control:*	Low.
Uses:	Develop concepts, principles, and facts in "how it works." Give directions of "how to do it."

LARGE GROUP STRATEGY 8

MOVIE, SLIDES, TV, RECORDINGS

Definition:	Media presentations which are similar to a lecture in that they present content without student feedback at a predetermined pace. These media supplement the verbal dimension of the lecture to add visual or audio capability.
Current Use:	Poor. Television is not used to the extent of its unique strength: immediacy of events. It is seldom used in most places. Overused to duplicate what other media can do. Other media can create superior sensory impact but are not always used to full advantage. Modern students are exposed to high technical quality media in their private lives; too often the school is a poor competitor with Walt Disney quality.
Planning:	More difficult than one would expect. All media should be previewed and shown at the proper point in the plan. Don't use media as filler for slow days. Don't use media without a specific reason.
Student *Involvement:*	Not as high as teachers expect.
Motivation:	About the same as the lecture unless the topic and/or quality is unusual.
Teacher *Content Control:*	Very little during showing unless the teacher has the courage to stop the presentation at appropriate points.
Student *Content Control:*	Virtually none.
Uses:	Many and varied, but limited to overview types of instruction.

LARGE GROUP STRATEGY 9

DRAMATIC PRESENTATION

Definition:	A play, playlet, or incident acted out by students for other students.

Current Use:	Infrequent.
Planning:	Considerable. The precise amount of planning depends upon the nature of the presentation.
Student Involvement:	Rather high for students who are the audience and nearly maximum for players.
Motivation:	High. Drama is of interest to nearly everyone, and when students see students controlling the lesson interest really rises.
Teacher Content Control:	Strong as director of the presentation.
Student Content Control:	Weak if student is in audience. Strong if part of performance.
Uses:	Factual, concept and affective outcomes for students. Do not just have students perform existing scripts. Have a team of students prepare the entire presentation. Or, the teacher can have one group of students prepare a script and another group perform. Finally, this format can be used for role play techniques by outlining parts but not writing scripts. This method is a good alternative to the often used method of debating old issues.

SMALL GROUP STRATEGY 1

STUDY-REVIEW

Definition:	An activity for small groups of students (two to six) in which they are encouraged to review content and study together.
Current Use:	Infrequent. Typically, students are forced to study in isolation, and too often the teacher fails to take advantage of the students' ability to teach each other.
Planning:	Simple. The students, as they work, identify specific areas to pursue. The teacher's task is limited to selecting groups which work well together and selecting content.
Student Involvement:	Good. There are always students who are hard to reach, but this method will reach most pupils. Remember, students will do things for each other they will not do for their teacher.
Motivation:	Good. See Student Involvement.
Teacher Content Control:	Minor. Since this is a review method, the teacher has previously had strong content control and the time has come to serve as a consultant to the study groups rather than as controller.

Student *Content Control:*	Strong. Students are free to seek out what they do not know without being unnecessarily exposed.
Uses:	Review and reinforcement.

SMALL GROUP STRATEGY 2

DRILL GAMES

Definition:	Games designed to reinforce facts or concepts in a competitive atmosphere.
Current Use:	Infrequent. This method is well known to elementary teachers but is underrated by secondary teachers.
Planning:	The teacher can usually plan to have the entire class participate at once. Difficult if the teacher tries to build a new game. Manageable if the teacher varies the format of a game he is familiar with. Look at TV shows and simple games like Tic Tac Toe and vary them. Be careful to assure that the level of the game matches the sophistication of the students. Perhaps modification of adult party games would meet the purpose.
Student *Involvement:*	High. Everybody enjoys games and a comparison of interest level between scat work drill and games is entirely in favor of games for most purposes.
Motivation:	High. Seat work drill motivation is based on the students' desire to learn while the game adds the competitive motivation.
Teacher *Content Control:*	High, by means of game design.
Student *Content Control:*	Low, except when teacher asks students to design the game.
Uses:	For content reinforcement and for class morale.

SMALL GROUP STRATEGY 3

TASK GROUPS

Definition:	Small group activities (two to six) designed for students to produce some tangible result. Laboratory sessions, group reports, and various group projects fit this category.
Current Use:	Minimal. Few teachers recognize the strengths in permitting content development through small groups.

Planning:	Simple. The teacher must select the members of the group and the topic area as well as the work style (laboratory, library research, etc.); thereafter, the teacher serves as advisor to the groups to help them move beyond their procedural problems. Since there is a goal for each group, the teacher can keep several groups going at once.
Student Involvement:	High
Motivation:	For able students, very high. For other students, the assignment must be modified. Some students will have to be taught how to study with a group. However, motivation for the less able students will be raised by working with peers over the traditional lecture methods.
Teacher Content Control:	Varies according to the structure of the assignment.
Student Content Control:	Varies according to the structure of the assignment.
Uses:	Nearly any content development or investigation process.

SMALL GROUP STRATEGY 4

BRAINSTORMING

Definition:	A freewheeling session in which the participants suggest possible solutions to a problem without discussing or critiquing the suggestions. The only desired result of the session is to produce a list of ideas to be investigated later.
Current Use:	Minimal in class. Teachers have used it in certain situations without full awareness of the method. An example frequently seen occurs in school clubs is on the topic of, "How will we raise $500 for the club treasury?"
Planning:	Simple. The students are given a problem and asked to suggest solutions. A list is compiled of the suggestions. The process works best in groups of four to eight, which encourage full participation. Planning is easy for teachers who have already established an open climate in their classes.
Student Involvement:	High.
Motivation:	High.
Teacher Content Control:	None.
Student Content Control:	High.

Uses:	As a first lesson in a series. Brainstorming produces data that can later be investigated. Without follow-up sessions, brainstorming will not go anywhere.

SMALL GROUP STRATEGY 5

DISCUSSION

Definition:	Student discussions in small groups with some definite goal.
Current Use:	Infrequent.
Planning:	Moderately difficult. See Large Group Strategy 4. If teacher-led discussions are too often bull sessions, then you can see that small group discussions without teacher presence can be harder to plan. Perhaps a series of questions to discuss can assist each group in staying on the topic.
Student Involvement:	Very good, even better than large group discussion.
Motivation:	For some students motivation to study is heightened while other less interested students will use the opportunity to discuss other subjects.
Teacher Content Control:	Lower than large group discussion but can be improved with good planning and the use of feedback mechanisms such as a large group reporting session or student recorded notes on the content of the session.
Student Content Control:	Strong.
Uses:	Not for in-depth development of content in the cognitive domain. Very good for affective topics and for sharing progress on individual student projects.

SMALL GROUP STRATEGY 6

SOCRATIC METHOD

Definition:	First used by Socrates, this technique consists of the teacher sitting with a small group of students and presenting content by means of questions which encourage student thinking. See pp. 132–33 for the section on the Socratic Game.
Current Use:	Infrequent. Teachers often loose patience and tell the answer prematurely.

Planning:	Difficult. The teacher is limited to working with one group of four to six students so the rest of the class must have an alternate activity. A few teachers use this technique with large groups, but it is more difficult. The teacher must anticipate in his plan a series of questions leading to a conclusion, plus questions to bring students back into the logical path if they digress.
Student Involvement:	High.
Motivation:	Usually good by virtue of participation and teacher concern for what students are thinking about each phase of the topic.
Teacher Content Control:	Good. This is not a discussion and student answers are relatively short. The questions determine content.
Student Content Control:	Moderate. The students must stay on the teacher's topic, but they can work from what they know about the topic.
Uses:	Very extensive and especially good for content development.

SMALL GROUP STRATEGY 7

SIMULATION AND ROLE PLAY

Definition:	A family of approaches to instruction in which the small group learning process is controlled by the structure of the activity. See the text on this topic.
Current Use:	Increasing. Teachers fail to be clear about the goals of the methods they select. Too often these techniques are used only to change pace.
Planning:	Simple, if you use a prepared item. More complex if you make your own. Planning varies according to the type of activity used.
Student Involvement:	High.
Motivation:	Very good.
Teacher Content Control:	High.
Student Content Control:	Varies with type of method.
Uses:	Many and varied. See text.

INDEPENDENT STUDY STRATEGY 1

STUDENT RESEARCH

Definition:	Student functions as an independent investigator into a topic usually involving the use of the library.
Current Use:	Moderate. This method should be used more, but teachers often underestimate their students' investigative ability.
Planning:	Usually very simple. The teacher needs to plan topic selection to assure the proper focus for each student. The student should be involved in this process. The teacher needs to plan for the varying student abilities to locate material. Students often know how to investigate a topic but not how to investigate data sources. The teacher needs to be available to help students locate and organize data. The teacher needs to be clear in his own mind about the level of the product the student should produce.
Student Involvement:	High.
Motivation:	Mixed. Many students have not worked independently for years and may be afraid to do so or may have inadequate study skills.
Teacher Content Control:	High.
Student Content Control:	High.
Uses:	Most content development areas. Usually followed by a written report.

INDEPENDENT STUDY STRATEGY 2

LABORATORY

Definition:	Student investigation with the aid of material support into basic principles. Usually found in science and controlled by a set of directions. Language labs are not real laboratories but rather are media-supported drill methods.
Current Use:	Considerable. This method is well understood by teachers and is limited only by resources such as space, equipment, and materials.

Planning:	Simple. Using prepared workbooks or other materials.
Student Involvement:	Extensive.
Motivation:	Usually good.
Teacher Content Control:	High.
Student Content Control:	Low.
Uses:	Content development.

INDEPENDENT STUDY STRATEGY 3

SEATWORK-DRILL

Definition:	Independent student seatwork without contact with peers, usually on a set of problems or activities designed to encourage retention.
Current Use:	Excessive. Teachers use this method as an escape from lecture. The method can be helpful when the teacher is adept at finding students with problems and using the method to help them. Teachers would benefit if they realized that students can often help each other in drill activities and that on occasion task group activities (Small Group Strategy 3) are a good substitute. Bright students could be used to help slower pupils.
Planning:	Usually simple.
Student Involvement:	High until the point of boredom is reached; then low.
Motivation:	Varies with general motivation level of students. Here is one place to determine which students are unmotivated.
Teacher Content Control:	High.
Student Content Control:	Low.
Uses:	Limited to reinforcement and retention.

INDEPENDENT STUDY STRATEGY 4

PROGRAMMED TEXTS

Definition:	Program texts are similar to workbooks except that they have additional vital features. First, the work to be completed is

broken into very small steps to assure even student progress. Second, the programmed text gives the student a chance to check his answers as he works. Third, the program branches, giving the student more work when he answers incorrectly. Programs do not usually vary the working/learning style. They do vary learning pace and degree of reinforcement at each stage of the work.

Related Method:	Computer-Assisted Instruction (CAI) is essentially the same as programmed learning except that it is computer-based and gives more flexibility to the program.
Current Use:	Infrequent and growing.
Planning:	Very little. Programs take a long time to write so teachers simply use commercial materials in most cases.
Student Involvement:	High.
Motivation:	Often better than traditional methods like drill and workbooks, but motivation may fall if overused.
Teacher Content Control:	High.
Student Content Control:	None.
Uses:	Learning and retaining facts, concepts, principles. Can be used to speed up routine learning to provide more overall flexability in class planning. The completed student program can be assessed.

INDEPENDENT STUDY STRATEGY 5

STUDENT READING

Definition:	Student independently studies assigned readings.
Current Use:	Excessively tied to only one source, the text. Excessively forced into this single pattern.
Planning:	Having students read the text is a common method which requires little planning. With a little imagination, the teacher can improve on the method by having students read from wider sources such as library books, paperbacks, and periodicals. Innovative planning on having students share their readings in pairs, small groups, and as a class, as well as having them analyze the more important points in their reading, can breathe new life into an old method.
Student Involvement:	Wide variation in level of involvement (see Motivation).

Motivation:	High for able students on topics of interest to them, dropping to near zero according to overall academic ability, interest in topic, and study skills.
Teacher *Content Control:*	High.
Student *Content Control:*	Varies according to degree of student involvement in deciding the specifics of the reading assignment.
Uses:	Content development in most areas. Can be used for motivational purposes with able students. Attitude and opinion development uses are effective for good readers.

INDEPENDENT STUDY STRATEGY 6

STUDENT WRITING

Definition:	A family of learning activities in which the main focus is on student writing.
Current Use:	Extensive in the traditional student writes-teacher grades fashion. Many innovations are ignored.
Planning:	Simple. Students need a lot of writing experience since written expression is vital to their future functioning as educated people. Be careful to vary the format. Simple things that are often not done enough are to encourage students to rewrite papers after a period of time. Remember, students are often capable of helping each other, so try some activities in which students edit the work of others. Also, try team writing exercises to get students to discuss what they are trying to say as they create a team composition.
Student *Involvement:*	High.
Motivation:	Varies according to ability and past success as a writer. For many students you will have to draw them into the process. Perhaps some of the comments on the planning (above) would help these students. Perhaps small group writing games would help as well (see text).
Teacher *Content Control:*	Moderate.
Student *Content Control:*	High.
Uses:	Skill of expression, reinforcement of content covered, and ongoing motivation for the most able students. An assessable mode of instruction.

PERSONAL TEACHING STRATEGY 1

PERSONAL TEACHING STRATEGY 2

PERSONAL TEACHING STRATEGY 3

PERSONAL TEACHING STRATEGY 4

Problem 19—Selecting Teaching Strategies

19-1.   (Task Groups of Four to Six)

Your task is to examine and analyze the various strategies presented in the Teaching Strategy Selector. Select three pairs of strategies that appear to be closely related in terms of their potential use. One pair should include a large group strategy and a small group strategy. The second pair should include a small group strategy and an independent study strategy. The third should include a large group and an independent strategy. Answer the following questions about *each* pair of strategies.

1. Other than the different group size, what are the main differences between the two strategies?
2. What do these differences imply as you plan a lesson and make a choice? Describe the nature of the lesson types each method best fits.

19-2.   (Individual)

Try your skill in using strategies in one of the following situations:

1. Micro-teaching
2. Informal groups in class or in your dormitory
3. Tutoring sessions.

19-3.   (Groups of Four)

STRATEGY SELECTION GAME

The aim of this activity is to practice selecting appropriate teaching strategies for particular situations and to gather feedback on your skill in making these choices.

Step 1.   Assemble in groups of four and select a second group with which your group will work.

Step 2.   Each person takes a piece of 8½" X 11" paper, selects a topic likely to be used as the basis of a one-day lesson in junior or senior high school, and writes the topic at the top of the page. Hand the paper to the person to your left.

Step 3.   Write a reasonable objective on the paper you receive which (a) is related to the topic already on the paper and (b) shows what the *student* will be able to do at the end of the lesson. Hand the paper to your left.

Step 4.   On the paper you received, write the ability level you prefer for the hypothetical class. Choose from above average (AA), average (A), or below average (BA). Hand the paper to your left.

Step 5.   On the paper you now have, write the grade level (7 through 12) you select for the objectives.

Step 6. Your group will exchange papers with the second group.

Step 7. You now have rather specific descriptions of four hypothetical lessons. As a group, select the best teaching strategy from the Teaching Strategy Selector.

Step 8. Return the papers to the first group and to the person who created the topic.

Step 9. Individually, write a paragraph which critiques the choice. Remember that a critique is based upon criteria you state at the outset. An evaluation follows in which you state why the strategy was a good or bad choice.

Step 10. Exchange the papers again.

Step 11. Your group, as a whole, responds to the critique of the strategy selections on the back of the paper. You may stick with your choice of technique or change it.

Step 12. Turn in your papers to your professor. He will respond to the quality of your selections so you may have some notion of the realism of your choices.

Problem 20

20–1.   Unit Plan (continued from Problems 17 and 18) (Same Teams as in Problems 17 and 18)

Your task is to complete the plan which you prepared in Problem 19. Before you proceed, reexamine the plan itself. You may need to revise it. Then select teaching strategies for each lesson in the plan using the format below. Explain how you will treat instructional set, developmental activities, and closure within each lesson.

Unit Plan	*Teaching Strategy*	*Lesson Details*
Lesson 1.		
Lesson 2.		
Lesson 3.		
"		
"		
"		
"		

20–2.   (Large Group Discussion)

The plans you have completed are reasonably comprehensive in terms of topics, goals, objectives, lesson breakdowns, and teaching strategies. Discuss the other kinds of planning you would need to do to assure successful lessons. Suppose a lesson failed to work. What kind of planning can you do to anticipate the problem? What alternatives do you need?

20–3.   (Large Group Discussion)

Discuss the following position. Teachers who do not plan tend to rely on the textbook and lectures because they have not planned to do anything else. It seems logical that planning can prevent this problem. The teacher who plans actually opens his classroom to more student participation. Student teachers who reject planning as a restriction on their future students are therefore in error.

Group Size as a Factor in Teaching

Your examination of the Teaching Strategy Selector has given you some grasp of the advantages and flexibility you can gain by using small group and independent study instructional methods. A general summary of the advantages and disadvantages of each group size may further clarify their characteristics.

1. Large Group Instruction
>   Advantage: The teacher is in charge and all students are supposed to be doing the same thing.
>   Disadvantages: Students learn at different rates and in different ways, but large group instruction forces them into the same pattern. Students have no chance to develop independent problem solving skills.

2. Small Group Instruction
>   Advantages: Interaction patterns are closer to student, permitting more involvement, better adjustment of pace, focus, and learning style to students. The teacher is often freed from the presenter role and serves as an advisor. Students develop group work and problem solving skills.
>   Disadvantages: Small group instruction takes more advance planning and some active counseling of students as they start each activity. In some schools the first few small group lessons will reveal that the students need to learn how to learn in this manner.

3. Independent Study
>   Advantages: Independent study is the most involved and active for students. It meets individual needs best in terms of content, and student work patterns conform to work patterns of most professional and scholarly adults. You become a scholarly advisor.
>   Disadvantages: You need to keep track of many projects. This method places a greater demand on material resources than either of the other plans. As in small group work, some students will need help in learning how to work independently.

Each format for instruction has advantages and disadvantages and should have a place in the curriculum. The teacher can handle these patterns of instruction simultaneously if he is skillful.

Final Notes on Planning

Planning can open up your instructional flexibility as well as student involvement and freedom. This occurs only when the plan is well thought out, provides for student involvement, and includes alternatives in case of breakdown. Planning needs to occur on two levels. You are well aware of the need to have a clear notion of what you are going to do and what your students are going to do. You also must know why you are doing it. Be prepared for the inevitable student question, "Why should we bother with this stuff?"

Simulation:
A Good Way to
Get Started

Advantages of Simulation

Simulation, gaming, and role play activities are among the most recent developments in learning theory. Properly employed, this family of methods deserves the special attention of the young teacher. They raise the level of student involvement, increasing learning and reducing disciplinary problems. This type of learning experience is enjoyable for students and is low pressured for the teacher. Furthermore, these methods parallel the problem solving techniques used in business and industry. Simulating, gaming, and role playing are not perfect methods, but they are very useful to the young teacher who wants to break out of the rut and create a productive class atmosphere.

Unlike many teaching methods, simulations take a great deal of advance planning and testing. This extra effort pays off in reduced pressure as you teach. In a conventional lesson, you pursue two tasks at once: presenting the lesson and observing the class. In simulations and other structured activities, the content is planned into the package prior to lesson presentation and your role is that of a facilitator and observer. The payoff for you is time to learn about your students.

Many teachers are now aware of games but are waiting for commercial materials before trying this group of strategies. They need not wait. A teacher can modify packages for use with new topics, make his own, or in some cases, a class can make its own materials. This chapter will introduce you to some of these alternatives.

The Kentucky Simulation Model

The Kentucky Simulation Model[1] defines the relationships between simulation, gaming, and role play by means of basic characteristics common to the entire group of

---

[1]The Kentucky Simulation Model was developed by a group of five professors at the University of Kentucky to assist effective communication about this family of methods. See Herbert K. Heger, "Toward a Curriculum Building Technology," *Educational Technology* 11 (December 1971).

methods. These characteristics will be developed in your activities so that you can use them as a basis for selecting, modifying, or creating activities to meet your own instructional goals.

For our purposes, the term simulation covers the entire family of methods, including gaming and role play. Simulation is defined as the "act or process of pretending." Persons participating in a simulation are actively doing something other than the real thing. *Any structured educational activity in which the participant learns by pretending is a simulation.*

One of the virtues of simulation as a family of instructional methods is that simulations are not real activities. The student can make mistakes without suffering serious consequences. This is the reason for the widespread use of simulation in aero-space and industry: one can learn without risk of harm or damage to persons or equipment.

Professional football is a game which does not fit our model. The game is played for business purposes, not learning purposes. A Broadway musical may be role play, but because it is played for its own purposes as a business, it does not represent simulation. Yet, *practice* for the football game and rehearsal for the play are simulations. These rehearsals involve pretending in order to learn how to handle the real situation.

While the entire family of teaching strategies known as simulations shares the common trait of participant pretending and the common purpose of learning, the variation within the group of methods is due to the nature and degree of structure in three dimensions: activity, environment, and participant latitude. These dimensions will be discussed in some detail.

The Activity Dimension. Simulation activities range from role playing to gaming. In role play the learner assumes and plays a role according to his *own* best perception. There is little external structure. In gaming, by contrast, the role a learner plays is externally structured by controls such as rules and rituals. Gaming can also be characterized as being relatively competitive and win-lose oriented while learner success in role play is less stringently measured.

Role play depends upon few rules and rituals, while the reverse is true for a game. The goals of role play are more flexible, in an activity sense, than the goals of a game. Win-lose and competition factors are minimal in role play but very important in a game. On a continuum representing simulation activity, role play falls at the "low structure" end while games fall at the "high structure" end. Student freedom of expression becomes more restricted as structure increases.

Few simulation packages fall at the end of the activity continiuum, but the criteria determined at the extremes are useful in analyzing characteristics of packages.

The Environmental Dimension. Activities can be conducted in environments ranging from completely uncontrolled *natural* settings to carefully constructed artificial settings which are *symbolic* of a particular environment. Game boards are symbolic environments.

Common usage of the term simulation often refers to the environmental dimension since the most sophisticated simulation techniques depend on a carefully controlled environment. Everything about a Link trainer, for example, is symbolic of a particular airplane. The symbolic environment is the heart of the Link concept. One cannot learn to fly a Boeing 747 with a broomstick.

The environmental dimension of simulation is especially important as a limiting factor in designing packages. A Link trainer is a highly symbolic environment representing an airplane. It is necessary and expensive to provide the environmental detail if the novice pilot is to learn effectively and safely. In this case, the Link trainer is less expensive than the plane it symbolizes and it saves the potential expense of damage to a real airplane. The driver training simulator is different, however, because such a simulator at Link trainer standards would cost more than an automobile without yielding comparable advantages.

At the natural end (low structure) of the environmental continuum are activities which need little environmental control or require only readily available environments. Twenty-one questions and many factual recall games can be played anywhere: symbolic environment is not needed. Environment is a minor factor in role play of various kinds of human interactions since people interact nearly everywhere. Rehearsing a play, by contrast, usually needs a stage matching the characteristics of the actual stage to be used.

As already indicated, highly symbolic environments are infrequent in educational simulations because of cost. Environmental factors, such as maps and charts, can be provided in classroom simulations. Further, a remarkable number of business and professional decision-making processes can be simulated because they take place within environmental structures similar to the structure of the school.

The Participant Latitude Dimension. Just as different activities can be conducted in different environments, so can they be conducted with different degrees of freedom for the participant. A future 747 pilot undergoes Link trainer activities to master certain well defined skills—a narrow *training* latitude—while an educator might undergo the same Link training under less rigid *experimental* latitude. The educator may wish to understand the *process* in order to design new techniques, while the pilot must master certain skills; the results desired influence the latitude permitted the student.

This dimension is the most difficult to control. How seriously will students take the activity? Will they buckle down to training latitude and master the skills developed in the activity? Or will they operate in the experimental mode? The answer depends upon the quality of the game, upon the peer group, and upon the manner in which you establish the need to take the activity seriously.

Some simulations should be played in the experimental latitude to permit exploration of the situation. It depends upon the objectives of the package.

General Notes on Simulations. Simulations can provide unique learning experiences for children. They provide active learning focused on decision-making processes rather than on drill or recall processes. Laboratory procedures are usually limited to following directions to identify and discover results of prescribed procedures. By contrast, simulations can encourage a student to choose alternatives and discover consequences on his own, thus making them more meaningful.

The weaknesses in most current educational simulations are (a) lack of clarity about goals and objectives and (b) lack of follow-through. Too often simulations are developed, marketed, and used because they *seem* to provide good learning activities. The evidence is often limited on how well the particular device affects student outcomes.

This is important, especially to a new teacher, but it is not enough. What is needed is a clear understanding of what the package is *supposed* to do.

Follow-through is important because most simulations give students the experience of making selections from a series of alternatives but fail to call the students' attention to the process by which they make their choices. What is needed for many packaged items is a debriefing activity in which students analyze the activity and link choices and consequences.

The choice-consequence link may not be important in activities designed to establish affective outcomes such as moods or feelings. The "Perplexity" game and "Black Angels" fall into this category. However, if the objective calls for going beyond the affective to an analysis of the causes of the situation, one must have a debriefing activity. In the case of "Black Angels" one can get a "feel" for faculty meetings by participating. However, causes of student protest and of a faculty's difficulty in reaching a decision cannot be identified without a post-session analysis.

"Black Angels" can also be used to build skill in faculty participation on the part of the student teacher. Here one must repeat the activity or a series of similar activities in order to reach the objective.

As in every other educational situation, it is up to you to provide the sense of purpose needed to make lessons viable. Simulations are no exception.

Problem 21

21–1.   (Individual—Commercial Simulations)

Locate and evaluate a commercial simulation. Your evaluation will be used in Problems 21–2 and 21–3. Try to locate items which relate to your teaching discipline. Remember that our definition of simulation includes gaming and role play. You are likely to find your sources in several areas. Do not overlook any of them. For locating complicated packages (such as Country X, page 190) you will find directories of simulation materials in the library. Publishers of these packages are not only textbook publishers. Do not overlook sources that appear novel, such as magazine publishers, churches, etc. Role play activities are often found, in professional journals or in books on the topics. Simple game activities are often available in books on a topic like mathematical games. Few high school texts include materials of this sort. However, since this is a rapidly developing field, directories may not cover all of your options. Writing to sources listed therein would result in up-to-date lists of packages available. Answer the following questions about the simulation you select for evaluation:

1. Does it develop an educational purpose through student activity or pretending?

   _____

2. What structure does it utilize? _____
   a. Activity: self-perception vs. rules _____
                 self-assessment vs. win-lose _____
                 low vs. high competition _____

  b. Environment: natural vs. symbolic _____

  c. Participant latitude: experimental vs. training _____

  d. Package objective _____

  e. Does the structure of the package help generate the kind of activity intended
    to reach the objective? _____

    Why? _____

    _____

    _____

    _____

    _____

21–2. (Groups of Four to Six)

  1. Share your findings in Problem 21–1. Discuss the potential of the packages. Try
   out a simulation or two if you can.

  2. Determine the appropriate use of your package with the help of the group.
   Describe that use below.

21–3. (Same Groups as Problem 21—Debriefing Activities)

One of the greatest problems in using simulations is linking the activity to regular
classroom instruction. The purpose of this problem is to build a list of methods you
may use to link simulations to subsequent instruction. List your methods on the blank
pages which follow.

 You may find it helpful to use the packages from Problem 20 as a basis for this
problem. The following hints may also be helpful.

  1. In activities emphasizing process or human interaction, student observers can
   provide feedback data on what happened for class analysis.

  2. In some cases, tape recording the class might provide data for follow-up sessions.

  3. These packages can launch student research activities followed by written or
   oral reports.

  4. Some packages need to be repeated, with or without rule revision.

  5. Not all groups within the class need to pursue the same package. This implies
   several points about sharing data on the experiences of the groups.

  6. Some packages get at skills which can be evaluated by test.

Develop your own personal list (pages 188–89) of ways to link simulations to regular
instruction.

Conducting Simulation Experiences

It is a relatively simple process to conduct educational simulations. You are usually
given directions to read to your students and they do the rest. However, you should
practice giving simulations in order to sharpen your skills in planning. You need to
learn whether the package really does what you expect. The following simulations are

SIMULATIONS-INSTRUCTION METHODS

included for you to experiment with. Try out one or more of these items in micro-teaching, student teaching, tutoring sessions, or in your dormitory.

You will notice a wide variation in purpose, format, and content in these examples. They all fall under our "Kentucky Simulation Model."

THE GROWTH OF COUNTRY X*

Geography: A Factor in Population Expansion

I.   INTRODUCTION:

This instructional package can be classified as a simulation. The students are asked to solve a problem which is realistic and which is similar to the kinds of problems faced by pioneering populations. The solutions proposed by the several student teams can be checked through comparison with actual demographic patterns. This package includes suggestions for follow-up activities which relate this problem to other disciplines such as art, literature, mathematics, and so forth.

II.   STUDENT LEVEL:

Junior or senior high ages. This package requires only elementary map reading skills. Solutions proposed will vary in sophistication according to the background of the students. This package can also be used at an adult level and is suitable for use in having pre-service and in-service teachers experience discovery techniques of learning.

III.   OBJECTIVES:

1. The students, as a group, will be able to develop a detailed pattern of population growth which takes into account the many factors of geography.
2. The students, as a group, will apply scientific problem-solving processes to a particular problem.
3. The individual student will participate in the group problem solving process and will sharpen his skills in observing, analyzing, evaluating, and hypothesizing solutions.
4. The individual student will, through the completion of follow-up assignments, develop interdisciplinary abilities in analyzing the impact of geography upon the development of a civilization.

IV.   THE PROBLEM:

1. *Task:* To project the population expansion patterns in Country X.
2. *Given:* General geographical data and specific problem-solving tasks to reach a solution which can be verified.

V.   DIRECTIONS:

Preliminary: As a preliminary step, review basic map reading and divide your class into groups of about five or six students.

---

*Created by Herbert K. Heger for use in his methods courses, "Country X" is a social studies simulation for four fifty-minute lessons plus introductory and follow-up lessons. To save space materials are included here for only one student group.

First Day

1. Give these general instructions to the class:
   1. This activity will last several days. It will involve class discussion, task group assignments, and individual assignments. I will provide material packages for your use.
   2. The purpose of this activity is for you to learn how geography influences population patterns and for you, as individuals and as groups, to learn how to solve geographic problems.
2. Let the students assemble as task groups and permit them to examine the packet of maps. Warn them not to write on the maps. Worksheets will be provided. (10 minutes)
3. Distribute Group Report 1* and give the following general directions:
   The country you are studying is now empty except for a town at X. Your first task is to describe the kind of people who are most likely to live at this site. Data on the nature of this town is on the GR1.
   Read the Report Form data to the class. Then, they should begin to solve Problem 1.
4. After about thirty minutes, call the class back together and discuss the results of Problem 1. Where groups have identified different answers to the first problem, all appropriate answers should be retained *unchanged* by each group. Groups with incorrect hypotheses should revise them. It should be emphasized that it is appropriate for each group to begin the next segment of Country X with its own set of hypotheses. *This discussion is a check on the processes of each group and it demonstrates how many diverse hypotheses can arise from the same data.*

Second Day

1. Class breaks down into task groups. Students begin GR2. Explain that each report form should have a map worksheet attached to indicate the stages of development for each group. However, you will not collect these maps until the end of the project, except for occasional checks. Students need the data from GR1 for subsequent problems. GR2 should take thirty minutes.
2. Call the class back to large group session and critique the results of GR2. *Be certain to develop the life support resource locations as a basis for evaluation. Then develop the preferences of the population as a basis for evaluation.* (15 Minutes)

Third Day

1. Students pursue Problems 4 and 5 on GR3. After twenty minutes have the total class critique selected results. *Do not take time to critique all the answers.*
2. Return to small groups for GR4. This activity sets the stage for individual written reports and follow-up activities you develop. Students do Problem 7 as homework.

---

*Hereafter, all Group Report forms will be referred to by initials only and numbers: for example, GR1, GR2, etc.

Fourth Day
1. Students discuss and turn in reports on Problem 7.
2. You develop follow-up activities over a period of one to four weeks. Groups can pursue certain topics or individuals can pursue topics. The possibilities are endless. Suggestions are given below.

VI. SUGGESTED FOLLOW-UP ACTIVITIES ON COUNTRY X:
1. The simulated area under study is actually a map of a portion of South America turned upside down. To compare this simulation to South America, turn the maps upside down and reverse January and July temperatures (Summer is in January in the Southern Hemisphere).

Students may compare their projections to the actual South American area. Be sure to discuss the fact that the simulation was with one *ethnic group* in *one empty country*. In South America there was a native population and exploration and immigrations by several nationalities. A look at the national boundaries would help with this point. Ask the students to consider how these factors might alter their hypotheses.

DOES THE ACTUAL LOCATION OF SOUTH AMERICAN CITIES CONFIRM THE HYPOTHESIS OF THE VARIOUS GROUPS? THIS IS A VITAL POINT. IF THERE ARE DIFFERENCES BETWEEN HYPOTHESES AND REALITY DETERMINE WHY.

2. There should be substantial follow-up activities to this simulation. The work can be individual or group, written or oral. Suggested topics listed below are only examples of the relationship of this simulation to all academic disciplines.
   a. How does Country X compare with the USA and USSR situations? What are the differences? What are the causes of the differences?
   b. Would the projections on Country X have been altered by the presence of political boundaries? How?
   c. What would a war after the establishment of two new towns have done to the other, later projections?
   d. What would a gold strike do to the projections? Example: The discovery of gold at the headwaters of River F after only two new towns had been established.
   e. Have the students discuss the effects of geography and expanding populations on the evolution of:
       applied mathematics
       manufacturing
       literature
       art
       religion
       social and health services
   f. What should be taught in the schools of Country X?
   g. If this activity is used as a role play activity for teachers, have them devise a series of follow-up lessons in all disciplines taught in school: science, math, music, physical education, etc.

VII.   PARALLEL ACTIVITIES FOR COUNTRY X:
This simulation may be used with public school students or with student teachers as a demonstration of pedagogical technique. Either way it might be advisable to assign one group from the class to the task of analyzing processes and evaluating products. This group would observe the small groups and record their problem-solving technique. They would take note of the relative success and accuracy in solving the assigned problems and report to the total group on the most effective process.

    This same analytical group could consider the various follow-up papers from the same process analysis view if the class is composed of student teachers. For the secondary school group, one would recommend analyzing all papers and selecting the best elements of each solution. This group would then construct an optimum solution.

VIII. EVALUATION:
Country X is an active learning device. The teacher can observe the learnings by observing the problem-solving processes and by evaluating the written results. A major learning outcome can be produced by having the groups switch completed report forms and maps and have each group evaluate another's product.

    Do not underestimate the value of having students identify some problem-solving processes they used in working with Country X.

    Do not overrate the value of evaluating the chosen town sites. Rather, focus on the reasoning process and the manner in which students chose sites and supported their decisions.

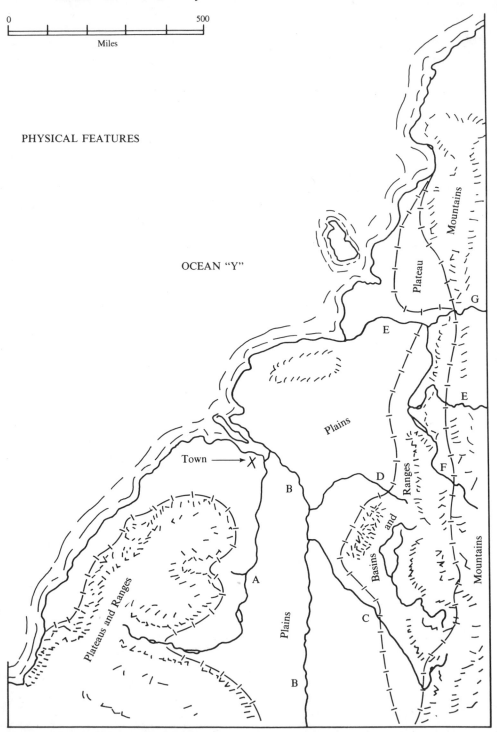

PHYSICAL FEATURES

OCEAN "Y"

A SECTION OF THE NORTHWEST COAST OF COUNTRY "X"

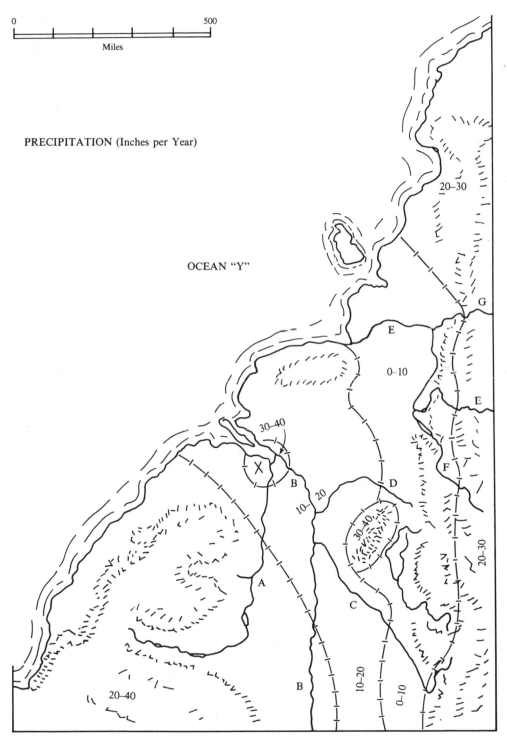

PRECIPITATION (Inches per Year)

OCEAN "Y"

A SECTION OF THE NORTHWEST COAST OF COUNTRY "X"

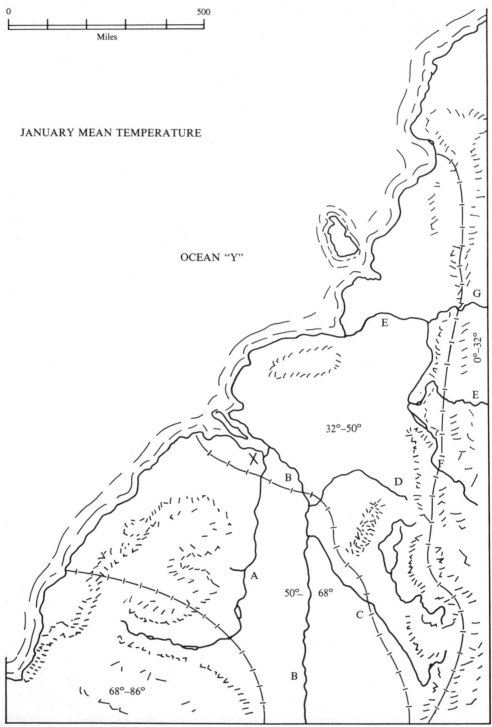

JANUARY MEAN TEMPERATURE

OCEAN "Y"

A SECTION OF THE NORTHWEST COAST OF COUNTRY "X"

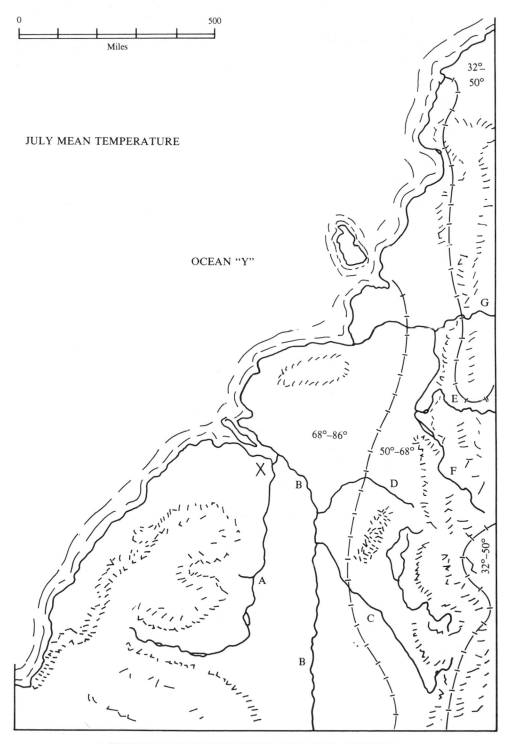

0 ———|———|———|———|——— 500
Miles

JULY MEAN TEMPERATURE

OCEAN "Y"

32°–50°

68°–86°

50°–68°

32°–50°

G

E

F

X

B

A

D

C

B

A SECTION OF THE NORTHWEST COAST OF COUNTRY "X"

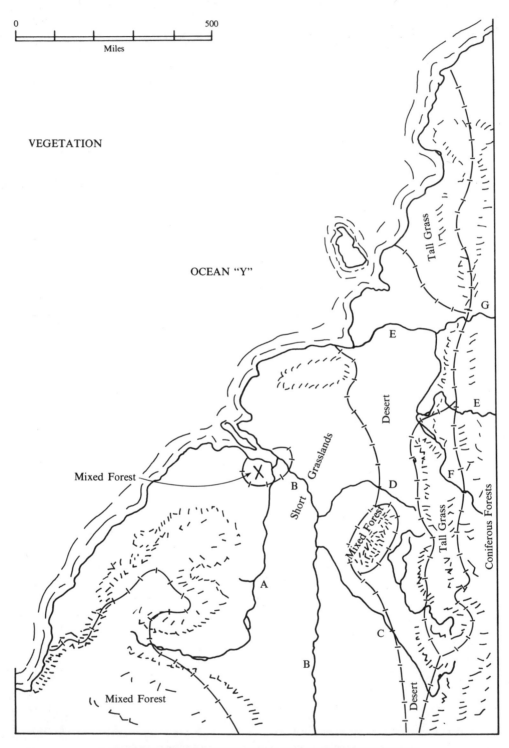

A SECTION OF THE NORTHWEST COAST OF COUNTRY "X"

Group Report Form 1

GROUP NO ——

GROUP   RECORDING
MEMBERS_____   SECRETARY _____

    _____

    _____

    _____

    _____

TOWN SITE:

Town X is on the delta of River A in an area of ample rainfall and fresh water. The natural vegetation is mixed forest although the residents of the community have cleared areas for farming and other purposes. The proximity of the bay is an important factor in the development of the community.

THE YEAR IS 1800. Railroads, automobiles, and airplanes do not exist. The steam engine and electricity are not available. Neither are the large-scale blasting and construction equipment we are used to. Except for these limitations, society in Town X is rather sophisticated in the European tradition.

DO NOT WRITE ON MAPS.

PROBLEM 1: Develop a set of hypotheses about Town X and its people.

   a. What land use patterns exist on the fringes of the community?

   b. What uses do the citizens make of River A and the bay?

c. Describe the town site and building construction and transportation patterns within the town.

d. What activities and interests do the citizens of Town X pursue in their work and in their recreation?

e. As the children of Town X grow up they will want to settle in lands and homes of their own. Describe the main directions which would interest them and the methods of transportation they could use.

REPORT BACK TO THE TOTAL CLASS AND DISCUSS THE NATURE OF THE PEOPLE WHO LIVE IN TOWN X.

Group Report Form 2

GROUP NO _____

PROBLEM 2: Locate the site of the first new settlement.

    a. What site are the migrants from Town X most likely to choose for their new settlement? Pick one site only. MARK THE SITE ON YOUR WORKING MAP.
       Site description:
    b. Why does this site seem appropriate?

    c. What geographical differences exist between the new site and Town X?
       Climate:

       Vegetation:

       Land Forms:

    d. What changes in life-style will the people of the new community make? What occupations will they pursue?

    e. Will the people of the new village trade with Town X? What kinds of trade will occur?

PROBLEM 3: Locate the site of the second new settlement. Consider the same questions from Problem 2 in regard to it. MARK THE SITE ON YOUR WORKING MAP.

    a. What site are the migrants from Town X most likely to choose for their new settlement? Pick one site only.

       Site description:

    b. Why does this site seem appropriate?

    c. What geographical differences exist between the new site and Town X?

       Climate:

       Vegetation:

       Land Forms:

    d. What changes in life-style will the people of the new community make? What occupations will they pursue?

    e. Will the people of the new village trade with town X? What kinds of trade will occur?

REPORT BACK TO THE ENTIRE CLASS. CRITIQUE THE CHOICE OF SITES MADE BY EACH GROUP. FOCUS ON THE PRESENCE OF RESOURCES TO SUPPORT LIFE IN THE MANNER THE SETTLERS DESIRE. REMEMBER, THE SETTLERS ARE NOT FORCED TO LIVE IN A SPECIFIC SPOT.

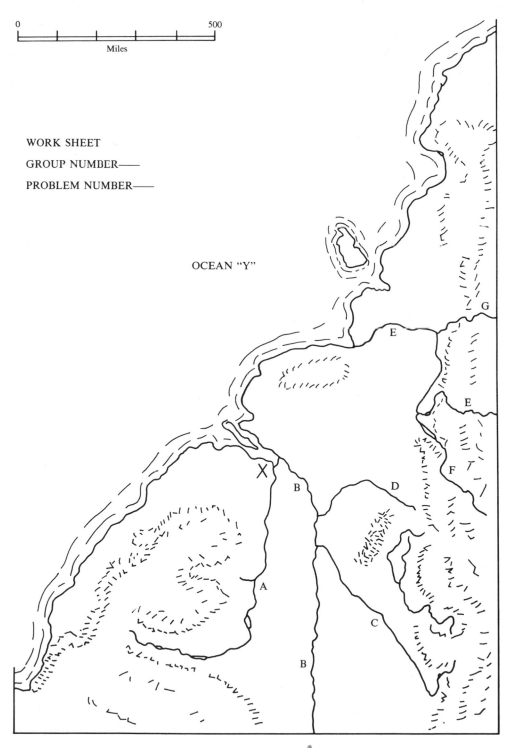

0   500
Miles

WORK SHEET

GROUP NUMBER——

PROBLEM NUMBER——

OCEAN "Y"

A SECTION OF THE NORTHWEST COAST OF COUNTRY "X"

Group Report Form 3

GROUP NO ___

PROBLEM 4: Select, in order, the next six town sites and justify your selection. Mark the sites on your working map

New Town Number	Site Description	Reasons for Selection
3		
4		
5		
6		
7		
8		

Group Report Form 3

GROUP NO ____

PROBLEM 5: List the means of food production, the most likely trade pattern, and the kind of manufacturing for each new town.

Town No.	Food Production	Trades With Which Towns	Manufactures
1			
2			
3			
4			
5			
6			
7			
8			

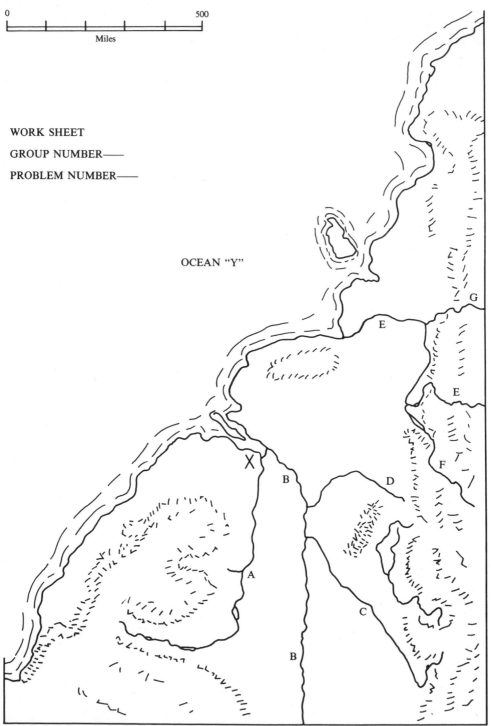

WORK SHEET

GROUP NUMBER——

PROBLEM NUMBER——

OCEAN "Y"

A SECTION OF THE NORTHWEST COAST OF COUNTRY "X"

Group Report Form 4

GROUP NO ——

PROBLEM 6:   Discuss how the cultures would *change* in the various new towns you have established. Be sure to exchange ideas regarding the following elements of the lives of the people:
> work
> recreation
> health
> physical activity
> culture
> literature
> education
> economic level

PROBLEM 7 (Homework):   Individually, select sites for:
> a national capital
> a banking center
> two university sites
> an agricultural college site

Write a paper justifying your selections. Mark the sites on your individual working map.

0   500

Miles

WORK SHEET

GROUP NUMBER——

PROBLEM NUMBER——

OCEAN "Y"

G

E

E

X

F

B

D

A

C

B

A SECTION OF THE NORTHWEST COAST OF COUNTRY "X"

SPACE CRISIS

"Space Crisis" is a simulation activity which deals with problems associated with value conflicts. Students are asked to role play a situation in which certain basic human values come into conflict, a situation compounded by pressure. The object is to role play enough of the crisis to realize that value conflict is real and that decisions made in this situation might not be approved in other situations.

1. *The Task*
   Role players are asked to consider the problem presented in their mythical situation and to decide on a solution which (a) saves the lives of the greatest number of people, (b) meets the test of conventional law, and (c) salvages the mission objectives.

2. *Directions*
   a. Designate astronaut teams of five persons. Command Pilot: He is legally in charge, can issue orders, and is the only person capable of flying the space ship. Co-Pilot: Mortally wounded, he is able to participate in the decision but is expected to die within a week. Flight Engineer: He is capable of repairing the ship and of directing others to assist in repair processes. Geologist and Physicist: These men have no skills in space flight, but they are needed in order to achieve the data collection which is the mission purpose.

3. *Rules*
   a. The rules are essentially those which govern any human group in a crisis. The Command Pilot is authorized to give orders, but the crew may disobey. The group knows that traditional legal values will be upheld at home.
   b. There is a fifteen minute time limit.

4. *Role of the Observer*
   An observer should be appointed for each group. The observer will lead the debriefing discussion. Points to be discussed include:
   a. The participation process.
   b. The practicality of the solution reached.
   c. The nature of the decisions made. Did the group face up to the value decisions involved?
   d. Was the decision consistent in terms of values expressed?
   e. Critique the values applied in the solution.

5. *The Problem*
   The space crew is stranded on the surface of the moon near an alien space ship. There is no communication available to earth and no communication possible to the aliens. There are two aliens and it would be possible to overpower them for their oxygen supply if necessary. The space crew has a food supply problem, but the oxygen supply is more critical. The space crew cannot expect help from earth.

a.   It will take nine days to repair the ship if the payload is retained. If the payload and mission purpose is abandoned, repair time is only eight days.
b.   Travel time to earth is six days.
c.   Oxygen for six days for all five crew members is on the space capsule orbiting above.
d.   The lunar lander is equipped with an oxygen supply of three days per man or a total supply of fifteen man/days of oxygen.
e.   The two aliens have a five day oxygen supply each or a total supply of ten man/days of oxygen.

Who should live and who should die?

Should the co-pilot be killed?

Should the aliens be killed?

What should be done about the payload?

What about the legal and moral implications of your likely court appearance?

TRYING TRIANGLES

"Trying Triangles" is a game for the development of communication skills and the spirit of cooperation necessary for success in team enterprises. This activity is effective with only one team or it may be conducted with several teams competing to solve the problem in the shortest time.

Preparation:

1. For each team involved, prepare six identical triangles. Cut each triangle into smaller pieces. Be careful to make sure that there are several options on reassembly of mixed parts which produce perfect triangles in one or two cases and odd pieces in the other cases.
2. Mix the triangle parts and put them into six envelopes assuring that each envelope has the same number of parts.

Directions:

1. Each member of the team receives an envelope.
2. Team members *may not* talk.
3. Through the use of nonverbal communication, the team members swap parts in order to build their personal triangle.
4. Team members may refuse to trade pieces if they wish.
5. Do not tell participants about the impending breakdown in the process. Usually one or two people complete their triangles and withdraw from trading, leaving the rest of the group with odd, useless parts. There is often considerable internal tension until the people with complete triangles realize that they must give up their triangles before all can complete their triangles.
6. Often the use of an observer to analyze the process is helpful.

Problem 22—Testing Simulations

Try one of the preceding simulations in micro-teaching, tutoring, or in your dormitory and report on the experience. Submit your report to your instructor.

22–1. (Individual)

How well did you do in presenting the activity?

22–2. (Individual)

What would you change if you repeated the activity?

22–3.   (Individual)

Discuss where you would use this activity and how you would prepare follow-up lessons.

Changing the Purpose of Simulations

Often the easiest way to develop a package of your own is to alter the content and format of an existing package. The author pursued this method as this text neared the press deadline with "Black Angels," in which you participated earlier. The activity emerged from a student protest over the Vietnam War which occurred in a Hawaiian high school. The role play package which was created was called "Aloha High School" and was used for several years in the author's methods classes. As press time neared, Vietnam began to recede as a topic of protest while racial injustice remained an important issue. Since the point of the activity was the difficulty that faculties have in reaching accord, it was decided that the structure and situation should remain the same, while the protest issue should be revised.

The structure of "Black Angels" fits nearly any school protest issue. If one wanted to revise the activity to cover a new issue, it would have to be rewritten to cover the new issue and the various perceptions faculty members are likely to have. The format, however, would remain the same.

Problem 23—Modifying Simulations

23–1.   (Teams of Two)

Examine "Black Angels." How would you change it to cover another issue? Pick a new issue and rough out a draft of the new activity. Possible issues include parental revolts on busing to achieve integration, revolts over sex education, student riots at school events, protests over unauthorized search of lockers, and so on.

Another alternative is to use this format for a council of war situation. When does the group decide to fight?

23–2.   *(Teams of Two)*

Revise the "Space Crisis" activity presented earlier to cover another situation. Keep the structure and elements of the activity concerning isolation. Change oxygen supply problems to food or water problems. Possible topics include situations occurring when men are lost at sea, trapped in a mine, or isolated in the wilderness. The famous Donner Party incident during the California gold rush would be a good topic.

Building New Packages

The creation of completely new simulations is not difficult as long as you have a clear notion about your objectives and the kind of action you wish to occur. Perhaps the easiest next step is to choose a format from another package which seems to meet your objectives. From this point on it is a matter of trying the activity with several groups as you create the bits and pieces of your package.

Always remember that the game structure is to enable, not to hinder. Rules help the students understand what to do. Keep them to a minimum and alter them freely.

Game Building Procedure

1. Select topic.
2. Determine objectives.
3. Select participant action desired.
4. Determine criteria for success and whether a win-lose factor is needed.
5. Determine how much participant latitude is appropriate.
6. Determine the materials students need to work with.
7. Create or borrow a format for the activity.
8. Assemble the package.
9. Test the package.
10. Refine the package.

Problem 24—Honors Problem

Build your own game. You may work alone or in groups. The author has encouraged his students to create their own activities in his courses, and a surprising number of students have accomplished the task. One student built a game in the "Monopoly" format to deal with the problems of the rural poor. Another developed an activity in which rival student teams could trade for paper clips and other trivia or could get these materials faster by going to war. His project was a remarkable demonstration in the operation of human competition and greed.

Miscellaneous Game Ideas

1. A Punctuation Drill Game
   Teams punctuate on a competitive time basis. Sentences used seem to lack sense but can be made reasonable.
   Example: "In a school examination Mary where Jane had had had had had had had had had had had the teacher's approval."
   Answer: In a school examination, Mary, where Jane had had "had had," had had "had." "Had had" had had the teacher's approval.

2. A Vocabulary Development Activity
   Individual students compete for points.

    a. Shortest synonym to word wins point.

    b. Longest synonym to a word wins point.

3. Sentences with missing words.

4. Poetry with missing words.

5. A Game Developing Observation, Analysis, and Problem Solving Skills
   Teacher to Student Group (four to six people): "John and Mary are dead. They are lying on the floor. There is a puddle of water and broken glass on the floor. Who are John and Mary and what happened?" First one with correct answer wins (even without rule).
   (Answer: John and Mary are goldfish and their bowl tipped over.)

6. A Math Skill Game
   Revise card games like "Black Jack" or "21" to develop fraction skills. Cards have fractions on them instead of the usual whole number values for Kings, treys, etc. The game limit is one rather than twenty-one.

7. A Game Format Developing Recall
   Competitive team question-answering events.

    a. Question by question, team gets point for correct answer.

    b. All questions answered at once, on paper, by each team. Score is determined by time taken to answer. Fifteen seconds is added for each wrong answer. Lowest score wins.

Final Notes on Simulations

Simulations are not a perfect answer to all problems of teaching. The objective in this chapter was to interest you in trying a group of techniques which can help you break out of the rut of traditional teaching. There was no intent to make a game builder out of each reader, but it was hoped that you would begin to collect simulation packages and ideas *prior* to student teaching. It is hoped that advance planning and collection of materials will reduce the pressure as you enter the teaching role. Finally, it is hoped that you avoid overestimating the sophistication of the simulations you are most likely to find available.

7

Next
Steps in
Teaching

Change in American education is now a reality. Experts are currently unable to predict the precise shape of education in 1980, yet there are certain factors which will remain the same. One of these is the nature of the truly professional teacher. Many of his activities and duties may change, including his teaching strategies, but the "compleat teacher" will continue to be the same kind of person.

The compleat teacher is the mature, secure person who maintains his sense of perspective. He is the one who worries only about his students, rejoices in their successes, however minor, and understands that administrative trivia facilitates the learning process for all concerned. He is the one who sacrifices his personal schedule and priorities to help his students develop their self-concepts, personal priorities, and self-control by encouraging them to freely investigate, study, and interact with the scholastic community. He is the one who avoids playing "buddy" and limits himself to the role of advisor and scholarly guide as the students explore man's academic heritage and limitations. He is not an egg-headed showoff performing in front of his captive audience.

There are few compleat teachers in the profession. The aspiration of this book is to help break the pattern and give you, the aspiring teacher, a few alternatives in order to take the first steps toward a better, more effective professional role.

This has been, for you, an experience without final closure. You are beginning a long learning process. What are the next steps in becoming a teacher? What tasks should you pursue between the completion of this text and your first professional assignment? They are many and varied; only a few can be presented here.

The themes of this text have been built on the contention that young teachers are concerned about personal survival, and the related contentions that teachers cannot survive until they (a) reach their students, (b) develop realistic perspectives of what they can accomplish, and (c) develop skill in planning and teaching. It follows that you will need to continue to develop these areas.

*Successful teachers
believe in students. . .*

You need to learn all you can about students, what they think and how they act. You need to participate in informal discussions with them before and even during your teaching. You need to accept their questions about relevance, the uncertainty about the future. You need to know them well enough to believe in them and trust them.

plan intently. . .

You need to plan ahead using all the ways you know to get your students engaged in learning activities. You need to plan with other student teachers and in-service teachers to avoid the lonely desperation facing too many educators.

teach skillfully. . .

You need to practice your teaching and self-analysis skills every way you can. You need to micro-teach, tutor, and participate in any kind of instructional process you can. You need to tape record yourself regularly and check on the match between what you did and what you intended to do.

know they can. . .

Your goal is confidence in yourself and your students. Always remember that students will give you the benefit of the doubt when something goes wrong; students want pleasant experiences as much as you do.

*but do not take them-
selves too seriously.*

Always remember that experts are people who have learned what they do not know as well as what they do know. Always remember that some of your students may know things you do not know. Remain open to new ideas, especially when they come from students. Your students can help you become a professional.

Bibliography

Allen, Dwight, and Kevin Ryan, *Microteaching*. Reading, Mass.: Addison-Wesley Publishing Co., Inc., 1969.

Berlo, David K. *The Process of Communication*. New York: Holt, Rinehart and Winston, Inc., 1960.

Galloway, Charles M. *Teaching is Communicating*. Washington: Association for Student Teaching—N.E.A., 1970.

Gordon, Alice Kaplan, *Games for Growth*. Palo Alto, Calif.: Science Research Associates, 1970.

Hyman, Ronald T. *Teaching: Vantage Points for Study*. Philadelphia: J. B. Lippincott Company, 1968.

Jersild, Arthur T. *When Teachers Face Themselves*. New York: Teachers College Press, Columbia University, 1955.

Jones, Richard M. *Fantasy and Feeling in Education*. New York: New York University Press, 1968.

Mager, Robert F. *Preparing Instructional Objectives*. Palo Alto, Calif.: Fearon Publishers, 1962.

Popham, W. James, and Eva L. Baker, *Systematic Instruction*. Englewood Cliffs, N.J.: Prentice-Hall, Inc., 1970.

Sanders, Norris M. *Classroom Questions: What Kinds?* New York: Harper & Row, Publishers, 1966.

Simon, Anita, and E. Gil Boyer, *Mirrors for Behavior*. Philadelphia: Research for Better Schools, Supplements A and B, 1970.

Index